Goal
Organization
Motivation

By **Brian Ronald Waldron**

Copyright © 2021 by Brian R. Waldron
All rights reserved under International Copyright Conventions. No part of this book may be reproduced or transmitted in any form or by any electronic or mechanical means, including photocopying, recording or by information storage and retrieval systems, without the written permission of the publisher, except where permitted by law. Reviewer may quote brief passages in a review.

The intent of the author is to impart information gained through trial and error in a quest to understand the science and art of helping himself.

"This story is a poem of life in action. It is the sea I sailed. I hope your sea is filled with the story of life you tame."

Goal Organization Motivation
Copyright: Registration Number: 1180436
Registered: 2021-03-30
Published in 2022
Waldron, Brian Ronald
Goal Organization Motivation, GOM: B.R. Waldron
Issued in print and electronic form.

Hardcopy book: 978-1-7776709-1-7
Paperback: 978-1-7776709-0-0
Electronic book: 978-1-7776709-2-4

Author Photo – Lauren Waldron
Book Design – B.R. Waldron and M.W. Croxall
Editing – M.W. Croxall
Cover Design – B.R. Waldron and Adahlia Neil
Concept and Renderings – Adahlia Neil and B.R. Waldron
Cover Graphics – Adahlia Neil
Interior Layout – Robin Forsyth
Printed on demand

Contact information:
Website for **Goal Organization Motivation**:
http://goalorganizationmotivation.com/
Email: brian@gom-it.com

To Kathy
"I bend to pick the leaf of red,
As the leaf converts
I too blend into a place of peace.
Such is the magic of my life."

CONTENTS

9   Introduction

15   CHAPTER ONE
Getting To The Point

19   CHAPTER TWO
My Kayak Ride

29   CHAPTER THREE
Metaphors
Translating my logic

47   CHAPTER FOUR
GOM Evolution

65   CHAPTER FIVE
Goal

73   CHAPTER SIX
Organization

95   CHAPTER SEVEN
Motivation

117   CHAPTER EIGHT
The Tiny Picture
Detailed analysis of how I approach a new situation

133   CHAPTER NINE
The Big Picture
My application of GOM

159   CHAPTER TEN
The Future Evolution of GOM
Wrapping it all up

174   **Acknowledgements**
176   **Tall Mast**
178   **References**
184   **About The Author**

"Tom said to himself that it was not such a hollow world, after all. He had discovered a great law of human action, without knowing it — namely, that in order to make a man or a boy covet a thing, it is only necessary to make the thing difficult to attain."[1]

— Mark Twain,
The Adventures of Tom Sawyer

Introduction

It was a grand adventure to scribe this material over the last fifteen years. After writing chapter one numerous times, I gained an appreciation for how things might fall into place, if I only knew how to craft the story. Getting to that final place eluded me.

It's a fall day in 2018 and I find myself at a place in my life where writing this book is my clear **goal**. The experience is cathartic. The art of writing my thoughts makes them more tangible. With that in mind I determined that the book had to be simple and no more than 10 chapters, which seemed right. Don't ask me why?

I do want to give that which was given to me. So, welcome to the story of **GOM.**

GOM or **Goal Organization Motivation** is a system to assess a situation, reach a decision and formulate action. Three words act as a framework tied to knowledge, experience and intuition. This model allows a capable person to access complex situations and apply the system. Complex means knowledge or information has to be discovered.

The terms **Goal** and **Organization** are easier to grasp and articulate. This does not imply that they are trivial, nor fully understood. **Motivation** is more mysterious. It requires a solid understanding of what "sticks" the **G** and **O** together.

Through a mandate to teach myself to get to the point I struggled with defining levels of the necessary details to write this book. Gaining a crisper notion of flow and corralling editing skills to eliminate clutter is easier once the ideas are down on paper. I could make any short story into an epic tale, and I did.

It made me happy, although I knew I would lose my audience: a constant failing on my part.

There I was, ten chapters of writing and nowhere to go. Forty thousand plus words of my own making and not knowing how to bring them to life. For a viable piece of literature, I had the words and the idea, but no flair for the art. At best, my writing skills were in need of improvement. OK, my writing skills sucked and I wallowed, but not for long.

Out of nowhere appears a friend. Someone interested enough to sit down and listen to this great idea I had for a book. She asked if she could read it. Her curiosity and patience were admirable. She gave constructive criticism and constantly challenged my clutter, connecting dots in a way that made my story flow. She watered down my lofty ambition to be a great writer and gave me the courage to grow into a guy with something to say; I had a voice. The book assumed a life of its own and blossomed into this publication. Thank you Molly.

Personally, I think the link to the physical world provides a great backdrop for this story. I was in search of buried treasure and had to learn to craft my life metaphors into tangible examples. Parallels of which demonstrated both strength and weakness. That is the way it is for me.

Believe me, there were weaknesses, which allowed wonderful and sometimes painful failures. Let me "get to the point."

> *"Ever tried. Ever failed. No matter.*
> *Try again. Fail again. Fail better."*[2]
> —Samuel Beckett

It is in the grandest failures that a quantum leap of learning evolves for me. Sometimes the learning is instant. Other times it takes time to process and grasp. Eventually, knowledge accumulates and gains perspective, which morphs into wisdom. I don't mean this in an arrogant way. In retrospect I can say, "I am OK."

Human training allows repeated attempts to gain expertise.

Looking back, I give credit for my behavioural ethic to my family and community in Kirkland Lake, Ontario.

My upbringing, family life, and work provided key values that shaped my thinking. Values tied to community included family love, hard work, honesty, respect, loyalty, honour and care for others. I understood and learned men were men and women were women, different but never subservient.

Values tied to competition include winning, losing, pain, wisdom in doing, and wisdom in age. Love of art and music, knowledge about fairness versus equality, respect for nature and ultimately, respect for me came into play when I moved out into the world.

So here's the thing. I had no idea of how these values would fit together with a career. When I left home to explore the world, it took me years to appreciate how I evolved to realize the logic of having **goals**; the necessity of being **organized**; and the importance of seeking **motivation**.

I give credit to Northern Telecom (Nortel), who provided the training style needed to make me a better manager. I honed my logic over ten years and it was here I discovered **GOM (Goal, Organization** and **Motivation)**. Philosophical ideas were the realm of management gurus. I was not a guru. I went on to cloak the ideas in tangible ways to broader audiences in both factory setting and engineering environments. Both setting and urgency had to be understood in order to know how far to go with **GOM**.

On January 20, 2021, Joseph Robinette Biden was inaugurated into the Presidency of the United States of America. Even with GOM, I cannot offer a prediction on how long Mr. Biden will be President as the American people are equally divided.

The transfer of power is much to the chagrin of the previous President and his followers. The concept of a tainted election by a President is significant; it would imply that the same process falsely elected him in 2016. His failure to recognize a winning path led to his own loss.

As the accidental President he squandered the opportunity to move his country forward. On this subject I found myself asking what was his **goal**? What attributes made him capable of managing a country? What was his **motivation** to become President? I have the need to comment on the Republican **Organization**.

GOM is at play at all times when I meet people. It is a dance of history, language, and body language within my surroundings. In an instant, it creates a piece of logic that allows me to determine how to proceed. Gaining confidence in my intuition was the awakening that moved me from the logic of engineering to the art of managing me.

My intent is to share this simple tool that can help others recognize a connection between intuitive thought and practical life experience.

One day I'm riding a bike carrying my fishing rod and the next day I have gray hair. I am OK with gray hair because I am satisfied and accomplished.

Enjoy the acronym **GOM.**

"And at my feet eternity draws ever sweeter plans for me, I know why – I know why."[3]

Robert Plant, Ship of Fools

CHAPTER ONE

Getting To The Point

I was a hunter for a couple of years and discovered that I was more impressed with walking the bush trails and discovering new things. I understood the need to hunt and fish, it is basic in my mind. I did not see any reason for me to hunt so I traded my gun for a camera and attempted to capture the "feeling" of seeing something new.

As with hunting, I am not comfortable with the perceived notions of "managing" people. People are different and to gather them into a herd represents a hunting mentality. The conversion from a group into a team however, was an intriguing switch that piqued my curiosity, as a manager became a single member with a defined role.

Entering a career after university showed that my critical thinking and self-confidence were ripe for improvement. Luckily, I was hired into a company that provided an environment to learn.

Training provided by Nortel for their managers was exceptional. We read relevant books, took courses at local colleges and universities, participated in defined internal training, team building, and technical training.

I remember off-site weekend reviews in the mountains around Alberta and British Columbia. As with everything, there was a standard deviation of managers from mentors with wisdom and historical knowledge, to rookies. This focused time created a bond that ensured ownership, responsibility, and empathy towards peers. On such retreats, I discovered the "heart" of management.

It took me 10 more years to grow into being a good manager. I say "good" as I compare myself to exceptionally great managers who earned my respect. Clearly, I still had work to do to be "great" at the art of managing people.

As my mentors would highlight, I wore my heart on my sleeve and this was a danger signal in the business world. It became obvious other managers had attributes that would give them power over me. I can sugar coat my naïve logic, however, this statement gets me to the point. I needed something to help me assess others. Thus began the search to help me, help me.

> *"I eagerly entered a search to help me, help me."*

What I needed was something beyond updated business books disguised with current terminology and references. I dug into the research and began to see that better business books selected a sliver of science logic, and built their presentation around this single aspect.

I read the leading-edge science of the time. It was over my head but patterns and new ideas did take shape. I think specifically of a triangle, the basic frame structure of a street bike. The significance of this is relevant only to my personal path.

There are analogies that can be defined in a scientific way and then transposed to human behaviour and vice versa. This is not a trivial statement. It takes a solid grounding in science with a set of social science skills to see the patterns. Social science is parallel to hard science. Defining the mathematics and language to explain linkage and metaphors becomes the art of translation to articulate the message.

I took steps to refine my personal guidewords to be inward and outward looking. My initial list of six words (freedom, honesty, respect, care, hunter and commitment) required a scripted prompt that pushed me to simplify my process.

At Nortel, acronyms were a way of life. I needed three or less letters and their associated make up that I could easily remember.

I wanted to create a simple logic to help me understand the world around me. More importantly, I needed to help me get a better understanding of my own thinking.

What became a continuous adventure to validate was also hard work. I do not propose an instant solution. Quick fixes are illusive, not perfectly timed. The real value comes with the toil and silence to find the path. As my three words evolved I morphed and landed on a place that I could remember.

My three words are:

- **Goal**
- **Organization**
- **Motivation**

GOM took ten years to feel right. It encapsulated the idea of helping me solve complex people relationships or at a more fundamental level, solving problems and making decisions.

A visual model is shown below.

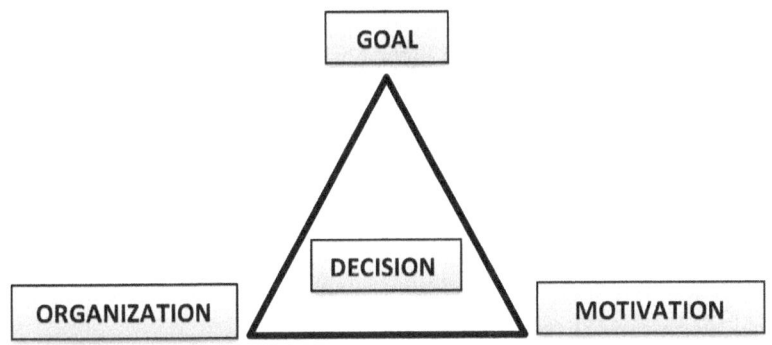

As a teaching tool this constructive triad can aid in the presentation of contrary positions, allowing others the option to define why they agree or disagree, highlighting a bias or exposing missing data and so on.

Are there holes in my logic? Yes. There are holes that hurt or embarrass, and others that take my breath away. It is the breathtaking discoveries that move me into action.

As a work in progress it is the "ah hah" moment that inspires the three words I am sharing.

One epiphany happened on a business flight while reading the book "The 7 Habits of Highly Effective People"[1] by Steven Covey. It occurred to me that these seven habits could be summed up under my three words. The earth-shattering discovery was my ability to see how the seven habits would fit as sub sets within **GOM**. I had advanced. I knew I was close. I could remember three words and expand them to assess any situation.

GOM would be constantly challenged with critical assessment of the logic. It was a complex challenge for me but it was the challenge that made the acronym stick with me. For now, three words are broad enough in capacity to act as headings for multitudes of other important words.

GOM became a memory process that I used in negotiation or management environments involving people. This was especially true in the work place where the rules of the game were general, and I had to make my way in the competition.

As people throughout my life gave to me, I want to give back and leave a nugget that I hope to be timeless. I will attempt to provide value and get to my point. I want to help you join dots.

"GOM stuck to me."

CHAPTER TWO

My Kayak Ride

September 27, 2018.

I am at the cottage on Rice Lake. It is a nice day with a light breeze and the place is rocking with Andrea and Matteo Bocelli singing "Fall on Me"[2].

The senate hearings[3] are underway in Washington for the appointment of Judge Brett Kavanaugh to the Supreme Court. Dr. Christine Blasey Ford has been called to testify today. For the first time in my life, I am engrossed in something foreign that captures my attention.

The Internet is streaming the events of the Kavanaugh/Ford hearings. I am surprised I am prepared to watch this process; government world activities are low on my priority list. So low, that it is a conscious decision to allow the "movie to play out" and wait for key sound bites that might produce answers. It also occurred to me, that this event tied to one president was about to redefine the United States of America.

To summarize: The Supreme Court is the highest court of the United States of America. It consists of the chief justice of the United States and eight associate justices. Each justice has lifetime tenure and when a vacancy occurs, the president in concert with the advice and consent of the American Senate appoints a new justice. The Supreme Court has the power to define laws for all in America. This team of justices utilize majority rule logic on acceptance or rejection of cases presented. It is a perceived advantage to appoint a justice who the president and senate believe maintains their assumed bias.

It is time for a kayak ride. I need to do something physical and clear my thoughts. The weather conditions are fine so I gather up the life jacket with river knife and whistle attachment and don sunglasses. The glasses are fitted with a float strap in case I end up in the water. Water shoes on, water bottle in hand, I set off.

To enjoy the ride to the fullest I would prefer to have a partner to share the experience. Today, I am good, being alone.

The kayaks are new this year and well used over the summer. Designed by a local company, the kayaks are a plastic construction, weighing in at fifty pounds, built for user height and weight.

Open water kayaking with wind and waves is within my experience level. I have never pushed the kayak to its limit, for example, tipping the kayak in water over my head and learning how to correct and get back in.

I approach the blue and black kayaks through a small grove of oak, maple and birch trees five feet above lake level. Unlocking the kayaks tethered to a large oak, I remove the fitted cover designed to keep the interior bug free. I peek. Who wants a dock spider crawling up their leg in the middle of a ride? Harmless yes, but we would both be trapped, and if either of us panicked, we would end up in the drink.

Inside the cockpit, I find the carbon paddles and snap them together. I retrieve the safety bailer from the rear compartment.

The lake is a foot deep at the water's edge. Stepping into the cool water, I set up the seat and lay the paddle over the width of the shell. With one foot in the kayak I twist to set my butt down. Drawing in my second foot, I paddle into the wind.

I had a thought that a snake or water animal might attack me. Being alone I wondered about my reaction and what I had for defense. Yes, silly drama, but that's me!

Another thought came, what if I tip? There are so few people around on this fall day that I need to observe my surroundings. A fishing boat appeared half mile away and I knew if I fell in and whistled there was a good chance they would hear me and pull me out. I modified my route to follow the shoreline. This new course would take longer but if I spilled out, I could walk to shore.

So what?

My kayak adventure is a simple way to expose the basics we go through every day to make decisions and move forward. My **goal** is to ride for one hour, travelling between the shoreline cottage resort and my cottage. **Organization** includes everything from safety equipment, kayak, weather conditions, water to drink, and training completed to get to this point.

My **motivation** is two-fold: to be active and healthy, and enjoy a one-hour ride viewing the cottages along my path. It is that simple. You might say almost intuitive or instinctive. I am confident a psychologist or seasoned kayak professional would find both good and bad in my actions. However, that is not the point. The point is, I defined my **goal**, and structured my **organization** to safely complete the kayak ride to gain exercise and enjoy nature.

One of the great things about getting away from daily structured life events is the time to reflect. It was in this one-hour kayak ride I thought to apply the logic of **GOM** to the senate hearings in USA. It is in this hour that I find a path to write a story explaining that logic. Eureka!

I come to my turning point and reposition the kayak to ride the wind. I sip my water as I idle allowing the light waves to push me towards home. At the midpoint, I am feeling good. With the island to the south and resort to the north, my surroundings are breathtaking. On the hill ahead, I see the summer home we own. It is tiny in my field of view but looms large in my memory. I am a mile from home and ready to return.

My paddle digs in slowly and with purpose. One stroke after another I start to gain momentum. It feels good. The air is fresh and the water pure. The shoreline guides my vision.

Imagine, a beautiful ride in a kayak and my thoughts turn to the U.S. senate hearings! As a Canadian, this is odd, even for me. My mind is heavily dominated by this event. Something is happening here.

I believe the senate hearings will act as a dividing point to drive the legal ethic into the future. It is about a position that will support the corporate mindset of North America. It is about men and women. It is about the presentation of two individuals and their statements about events that took place in high school. Who did you believe?

At this juncture, I believe Dr. Ford. My decision is based solely on what I have seen.

Kavanaugh's presentation was astonishing. What was the **motivation** behind the drama he created? That **motivational** data is what I searched for as I have little idea who Kavanaugh is. He presented his case leaving out pieces of his history he does not want exposed. The president had selected him. Did he have to put on a dramatic show of perceived manliness? He did not appear sincere. I could see his wife seated behind him did not believe him. I watched his testimony in piece-meal fashion. In my opinion, his presentation was suicidal. His bizarre manner had my gut sense tingling and the hackles on my neck raised.

Up to this point, I envisioned a judge as calm and direct, factual and relevant. My sense being, if he had wanted to put the past in the past, he should acknowledge basic truths. As a basketball player in college, I travelled the road and the behaviours I observed, and participated in, contradicted the data presented by Kavanaugh. Am I being judgemental? Maybe, but that is my opinion at the end of the hearing.

Over the next decade, I hope to discover the **motivation** for his testimony. I expect it will be buried until his day is done or there is a new President. I intend to research if a new President will remove Kavanaugh.

Wow! This is a profound kayak ride. What is happening here?

My thinking process is enhanced when I am in an open-air environment. I am breathing fresh air in a manner that floods my brain with oxygen, and yet, I am calm. The chaos of events begins to fall in order making decisions that have caveats. The caveats are pieces of uncertainty. I hope to flush them out over time. At this point, I do not know how the senate will vote.

I do have my opinion and I am aware that my opinion will be adjusted if a compelling truth is discovered. For now, I believe Dr. Ford.

Row, row, row your boat…I am making good pace across the water.

My mind adjusts and I take my thoughts up to a higher level. I will apply **GOM** to the selection of a Supreme Court judge? Let's try. I will use the data I have at hand: books, media reports, discussions with smart people, and my sixty plus years of experience.

My intuition is strong and my guiding factor. I have discovered I can trust myself.

"I trust my intuition."

GOM as applied to the USA Supreme Court nomination, by a Canadian guy in a kayak.

The **goal** is to select the best candidate available to be a judge of the U.S. Supreme Court.

The **organization** I will cover in a couple of high-level pieces of data.

The management of the government is defined by the U.S. constitution and selected by the democratic process, assuming no third party manipulation occurs. The parties are split by two primary camps, and biased in their own beliefs and mandates. Each one influenced by many, with money as the driver. The boss, the president, lies or lacks the ability to get the facts correct. Forgive my narrow scope here but I am in a kayak thinking this through.

"... a Canadian guy in a kayak."

Now, I have to figure out the tough part. What is the **motivation**?

What I understand is, the Republicans have to get Judge Brett Kavanaugh approved in order to gain control of the Supreme Court for the next 10 to 20 years. They realize that the primaries are likely to have them lose governmental power. They have to go for this long shot now, as their "house of cards" may tumble. Democrats on the other hand, know they may take power back and have to stall this appointment or live with the consequences they fear.

These are simplistic **motivational** statements. Am I correct in my thinking? Am I biased by fake news? Maybe, but this is what I have. My point is to provide an example, not to convince you of which path to follow. Do your own research to determine your decision on this topic.

I am close to the cottage now. I see the rock bolder dock we built, and I prepare to land. I begin to back-paddle to slow my landing and create an environment to easily step out and hold onto the kayak.

I step one foot into the water to stop my forward motion and rise to step out with my second foot. Placing the paddle inside, I lower the seat back, grab the handle at the front of the kayak and step out of the water. I ascend the rock steps and drag the kayak over the wooden slider boards to prevent damage to the shell bottom. After drying and cleaning, I cover the seat opening. Tipping the kayak against its sister, I lock them together. Job done.

Heading up to the cottage I feel both refreshed and firmly resolved.

That was one beautiful ride.

Let me take **GOM** to another level closer to home: How does **GOM** apply to the Government of Canada and legalization of marijuana?

To keep it within my own knowledge I will define the **goal** of the Canadian government to be the elected body of Canadians who define the environment for all people of Canada; to live in communities safely and freely, and to prosper as individuals. The **goals** are bigger than this, but humour me, please.

How is it **organized**? Elected members are chosen based on a defined bias or defined plan. The members process legislation that defines laws and policies that create environments for people, business, and public sectors to operate. Parliamentary procedures are utilized to debate and refine legislation, in order to refine the wording and make it applicable to public lives. Once vetted, a vote defines the passing or rejection of the legislature. I appreciate that it is more complex.

What is the **motivation**? How do we get at this somewhat emotional piece? The **motivation** is to benefit the majority and provide a better living environment within our natural environs. There will be deeper less obvious **motivations**. There are cynical aspects to my personal beliefs but let me keep it moralistic for now. It is up to each of us to process the data and make a decision on our own, to define how we will adapt.

Utilizing the government analogy let me define the legalization process of marijuana in Canada.

The **goal** was to legalize marijuana by the fall of 2018.

The **organization** is driven by legislation, parliamentary debate, and statistical limits in terms of safe application. Methods of distribution; tax collection; health benefits and concerns; laws to allow safe use and protection of others; public education; enforcement tools and education; and cross border implications are among the considerations.

There are unresolved issues. In the judgement of the majority government, unresolved issues can be defined through experience. The risk is considered low. Let me be clear, I am not advocating one way or the other. I want to build a metaphor in the application of **GOM**.

"GOM up in smoke."

What is the **motivation**? There are the defined medical benefits as laid out by various studies. This "seems" rational in the world of 2018. At a basic level, all medications are drawn from nature. There are other contrary forces at play. Could the legalization of marijuana interfere with existing public behaviours or norms? Is Marijuana viewed as a competing product? Will the competing product infringe on a market share held by cigarettes or alcohol products? I am not stating this as a fact, but laying out a **motivation** that could counter legalization.

The **motivational** part is the piece that creates the emotion of conviction that allows the public to accept or deny a presented piece of legislature. You can gather and process details on marijuana and its legalization. There will be positive and negative aspects. The individual who has a bad experience with marijuana will register in the public forum. For that reason, it is up to knowledgeable lawmakers and relevant medical professionals to ensure the benefits outweigh the deficits. It is then up to the individual to determine how it impacts them.

Determining the attributes of the **Goal** and **Organization** criteria is more apparent. **Motivation** takes a solid understanding of all the facts and logic used to understand why a position is taken. "Why" is the question that entices me to research **motivational** aspirations that are not as obvious.

As of Oct 17, 2018, marijuana was formally legalized in Canada. I believe this is a rational decision.

It is the **motivational** part that supports my decision to not use marijuana. I will leave it up to you to speculate on my personal **motivation**.

I'll have to do a deep dive and **GOM** the marijuana legalization on the next kayak ride.

CHAPTER THREE

Metaphors

Translating my logic

The kayak ride is my way of creating a story, and a set of metaphors that help me define the scope and logic I use to assess situations. To get to the point, I will simplify possible inputs, reactions, variables, luck, chance, effort and education, to create a piece of logic that has helped me.

Goal, **Organization** and **Motivation** (**GOM**) are three words that create repeatable memory logic used to assess situations that involve unfamiliar people or events. **GOM** presents a starting point.

Do we live a life in sound-bite **GOM** approaches? No. We do the things that make sense at specific times in our lives. As an individual grows and learns, the process becomes natural and intuitive in nature.

The kayak ride demonstrates the basics of a day-to-day task and helps explain how **GOM** is applied to the decision.

The **goal** of the kayak ride is to row to the next resort and back, in one hour. That is it. Do I make special notes or go through a rigid process to actually articulate the **goal**? No. The ride is a routine task and a repeatable process that requires minimal investment in the **goal** statement. It is a quick and intuitive decision. Simplicity is key.

- Do I want to ride?
- Ride where?
- How long?
- Is the weather acceptable?

The **organizational** part of the kayak ride is the heart of the effort needed to prepare and execute a plan.

- I am healthy and have done this ride 15 times through the summer.
- Training and practice have provided a level of confidence to believe the ride will be safe and successful.
- The kayak is in good condition, thus no fear of wear issues.
- The paddle was provided with the kayak and is set to the right position.
- Safety gear was researched and the appropriate pieces purchased; including life jacket, bailing pail, whistle and rope.
- A river knife is attached to the life jacket providing an option to escape in case I end up under water tangled in weeds.
- Preparation is a necessary process to standardize a repeatable pattern that I do once. Wear proper clothing, fill water bottle, remember sunglasses with float strap, don life jacket and retrieve key to unlock kayaks.
- I perform **organizational** needs to complete the task and paddle to a known target, which aligns with historic experience.
- Small, bite-size **goals** are defined along the route: go to the first cottage; water pipe; big cottage; water plane and big dock. Turning around, I reverse the order of small **goals**.
- Things happen automatically in parallel motion.

- I constantly look around to enjoy the view and to ensure weather conditions remain within my kayaking skill set.
- The ride is not a race. I have enough confidence to freely think about other topics. This lateral approach is something I enjoy and utilize on a regular basis.

This list of tasks could act as a flow diagram, initiating software development needed to program a robot to accomplish a similar task. Artificial intelligence is the marketing term used to humanize machine or robotic tools. The process of **organizing** is methodical and repeatable. The more the tasks are repeated, the more predictable the results become.

Nature will provide a level of random events, which stimulate rapid adjustments. In retrospect, it can force me to recognize that arrogance may have misguided the need to check the weather forecast! One kayak trip did trigger urgent action against a thunderhead closing in fast. To this threat, my brain re-adjusted quickly and decisively. Lateral thinking was curtailed and I focused on new, more urgent mini **goals** to move at a pace that would get me home before the storm, and to cover and lock the kayak. If I delayed another thirty seconds on the water, I would have been soaked or forced to land along my route to take shelter. I was able to get into the cottage as the downpour began.

"Repeated trials provide predictable results."

Failures are not a failing in the sense of a dictionary definition. They are events that force adaptation and correction.

Catastrophic failures can be studied to ensure corrections for future success. Engineering education in Canadian Universities remember failings of the past, offering graduates an Iron Ring[4] to remind its bearer of their obligation to the public.

Dramatic failure happens when an individual freezes in a crisis. For a brief moment they are stymied and do not know what to do. No one knows how he or she might respond until they encounter a dangerous situation. I am confident there are multitudes of examples where luck saves the day, or people act by chance in a correct or incorrect manner. An assessment would be that they do not have the skill sets to cope. I think specifically of first responders and the unique training they receive when faced with catastrophic situations. They process first and then act.

Goal and **Organization** are the tangible words used to define **GOM**. **Motivation** is the emotional piece. The **motivation** for the kayak ride is rather mundane.

- To exercise, because exercise is required to maintain a healthy body and mind.
- To enjoy nature at the cottage.
- To relax and think through current topics.

Motivation has a number of aspects that range from simple to cynical. It can be a complex piece of **GOM**, as I will explain later. The question why is heavily used to flush out **motivation**. Think of a court case. We get the details and may obtain the reason why a crime was committed. Or the reason why is never fully understood or explained. Missing the deeper reasons as to why a crime is undertaken prevents the opportunity to make wise intelligent corrections. Assumptions are then made and laws adjusted to accommodate potential misguided logic.

There were a number of metaphors in the previous chapter. The kayak ride was the story of a daily task. I will provide a second metaphor expanding on emotional preferences, before moving on to something more complex.

I grew up under the influence of music from the '60s. I remember the night The Beatles performed on The Ed Sullivan Show. A wise man told me that music starts at home, grows with time, and ends with jazz. It took me thirty years of listening to various genres, before jazz started to enter my life. Maybe, in another ten years, I'll be fully converted? Time will tell.

Classical genre was enacted in university, when I had to study for exams during hockey playoffs. Playing instrumental classics, I utilized the sound as white noise to drown out the boisterous commentary blaring on the main floor of the house. To this day, I appreciate periods of classical music.

> *"Music and poetry are creative forums that communicate powerful statements."*

The music selection rocking the cottage, "Fall on Me"[5] by Andrea and Matteo Bocelli is new music for me and instantly enjoyable. Why is it "instantly" enjoyable? How could that happen!

Goal:
- To listen and enjoy music that reflects my mood.

Organization:
- A friend recommended the music video.
- Awareness of the artists, their genre and talent sets a high expectation.
- Personal experiences of different genres are selected based on mood, situation, audience, and environment.
- Audio equipment is available with a good ability to reproduce the music projected by the artist.
- Software tools are available with access to the Internet and music content.

- Proficient knowledge and experience using the software is established.
- I utilize my cellular phone to play the video.
- The video caught my attention (visual, audio, and lyrics).
- To verify my assumption, I determine Matteo is Andrea's son.
- I hit the repeat button often to fill the air with the beautiful music.
- Studying the words in relation to the song and video. I am in awe of the power of the words and how they integrate with the video and the two men.
- A deeper analysis of the words resonated a number of themes:
  - Love between father and son.
  - Love takes effort.
  - An established and deeply experienced singing father.
  - A son with a more delicate voice.
  - Two languages utilized.
  - With reference to the phrase, "what is true"[5] the music reflected a positive side to the chaos of the world in 2018.
  - A blind father sings of "seeing you everywhere"[5].
  - A son sings of "breathing you in the air" [5].

The symbolism within the song is strong and understandable.

Motivation:

- A sense that I will hear and see something that will resonate within me.
- The music video is impressive and stimulates a desire to analyse the symbolism.
- The absolute enjoyment I experience listening to the song.

There you have it, two applications of **GOM** at a personal level. A kayak ride and the selection of music are daily tasks. The attributes provide insight, to set a scene. The music selection provides a peek at my curious mind and an emotional level of intuition.

Let's take this up a level and jump to the other end of the complexity spectrum.

The focus is on the senate hearings associated with the selection of a Supreme Court judge in the United States of America. The person under review is Judge Brett Kavanaugh.

My focus is on the final day of hearings[6]. Dr. Christine Blasey Ford is called to testify about Kavanaugh's behaviour at a high school party 30 years earlier. Kavanaugh is called to respond to the allegations.

The senate hearing analysis is complex for me. I will cover a number of issues under the **organization** heading. My intuition is telling me this is a historic event as well as a potential tipping point for the Republican Party, and the USA. This is the first time in my life I have watched any such hearings.

Goal:

- To watch the final day of hearings and create my own opinion on whom I believe.

Organization:
- I do not have in-depth knowledge of U.S. political bias.
- I do have a simple understanding of the Republican and Democratic Party's basic biases.
- I do not have intimate knowledge of the constitution, political system structure, or logic.
- My knowledge of American history is "twitterish" verses academic.
- I recognize that Canada is able to lean on the U.S. for military protection if need be.
    - This dependency has probably harmed all branches of Canadian military. In that, historic governments chose passive routes assuming we were a small, peace-loving nation. Yes, this may be true, but I believe we wasted opportunities to enhance our own military capabilities.
- I have high regard for the American people.
- I have neither regard nor respect for Donald Trump.
- I have researched background information of Judge Kavanaugh and Dr. Ford, as well as the details on the accusations.
- I have read the details in right- and left-wing papers.
- I have not read any of the documented testimony that is available to the public.
- I do have my opinions based on reading, and conversations with knowledgeable people.
- My opinions are biased, and I have to be aware of them as I assess the presentations.
- I have determined how to live-stream the hearings on my computer.

- I tune in to the hearings[7] and focus on the lead actors.
- Dr. Ford presents her testimony and is asked questions.
  - My sense is she looks terrified and sounds reasonable.
  - She appears credible and answers questions directly.
- Judge Kavanaugh presents his testimony and is asked questions.
  - My sense is he is struggling. I am shocked at his demeanour.
  - My intuition tells me he is in deep trouble and needs to deflect from answering questions.
  - I am shocked and I cringe. I have to stop watching.
  - It is unbearable to watch a person commit professional suicide.
- I skip the rest of him reading his statement and re-join when he is being asked questions.
  - Again, there is something horribly wrong with Kavanaugh's demeanour.
  - I am unclear on what I am missing.
  - I am suspicious of him and my trust for him is declining quickly.
- My brain is working hard to determine what is happening.
  - How does a man who is to be a member of the Supreme Court, avoid answering pertinent questions?
  - Why did he become aggressive and challenging with a senator?
  - Was he coached into this act? Was it an act?

- My summary is, he failed. He attempted to aggressively defend himself and to challenge questioners and failed.
- In the end, I absolutely (99.999%) believed Dr. Ford and absolutely (99.999%) did not believe Kavanaugh.
- Was I right? This was my intuition speaking, I have a keen sense for trusting my intuition.
- I may be wrong, but it will take strong compelling data to change my opinion.
- I will watch the news to see what is presented to the public from the FBI investigation, and how the Republicans and President handle the decisions.
- Subsequent to the live Senate Hearings:
    - An FBI investigation was narrowed in scope and the White House stated it could find no corroboration of the allegations against Kavanaugh.
    - Kavanaugh was confirmed to the Supreme Court on October 6, 2018. The decision was biased and driven through the majority Republican Party.

Motivation:
- My intuition told me this hearing is worth watching.
- I was curious to see if I could create my own opinion based on what was presented.
- My personal **motivation** was to gain an opinion and to experience this senate hearing.
- I did not suspect any Democratic conspiracy. The hearing was newsworthy and allowed speculation to draw attention to media headlines.

What do you think the **motivation** was for Judge Kavanaugh, Dr. Ford, Republicans, Democrats, and the President? To provide my opinion let me expand the scope briefly and speculate. I do this as an example of how I would approach a determination of **motivation**. My assumptions are biased, based on my limited knowledge.

> *"What motivated Kavanaugh, Ford, and the President of the United States?"*

Determining true **motivation** is difficult as I am not privy to the people and parties in question. There is risk of misunderstanding and creating error in a decision. My point is that the **motivation** of all parties has to be understood in order to understand the environment in which their decisions are being made. I do hope details will be provided publicly in the future.

Kavanaugh's Motivation:

- To save his chance at becoming a Supreme Court judge, and having a lifetime job and paycheque.
- To publicly deny the accusations.
- To verbally state and physically show, with passion, that he will aggressively defend his honour.
- To deflect answering questions or employ the "deny, deny, deny" logic utilized by the President.
- Did the President tell him to be "manly" or did he choose to act in the image of the President? He needed to assume a role that appeared contrary to his beliefs.
- His visual behaviour reflected a position in which he was defending the President and his Republican mentors.

Dr. Ford's Motivation:
- To make people aware of Kavanaugh's behaviour as a teenager.
  - The man, who was being reviewed for this prestigious position, had historic flaws contrary to the way he was being presented publicly.
- She was willing to risk her reputation and her family to expose her data.
- She was aware of public cases of abuse towards women by men, how the courts had ruled, and how public acceptance to her plight was more open.

Republican Motivation:
- To get a hand groomed judge, with bias towards party beliefs onto the Supreme Court.
- This position would represent a conservative bias to influence the court decisions over the next 10 to 20 years.
  - This bias would help manage a Republican agenda, and support narrow wealth control.
  - It would readjust public policy in favour of reduced social funding for the American majority, and support corporate agendas that create a greater concentration of wealth.

During the hearings, Republicans managed to limit access to Kavanaugh's past work.

The party as a whole was about to go into the November primary season and there is a good chance they may lose power in one or both governmental agencies (the House and/or the Senate). The risk had to be high as they tiptoed their way through the senate hearings by utilizing a woman lawyer to ask questions of Dr. Ford.

Except for one Republican senator who called for a FBI investigation, the Republicans knew they had to push the judge forward. It was all they could do to maintain control over the court system for the next 10 to 20 years.

Democrat Motivation:

- To want a more liberal judge.
- To delay the appointment of Kavanaugh until after the primary elections.
- To sink to the lowest of levels, as details pertaining to years of Kavanaugh's work were not made available.
- Win public opinion, especially among women, considering recent abuse cases against popular men.
- If the allegations are true, Kavanaugh might falsify his statements and be disqualified. This is a long shot with low risk and high visibility.
- To show leadership or a coordinated effort to deal with the Supreme Court Judge selection.

The President's Motivation:

- To have a judge selected who believed the President did not have to answer to the court for his behaviour or crimes as the sitting president.
    - To not be dragged into the court system for review of himself or his family.
- As a consistent liar in public he will have escape language ready to cover his personal selection of Kavanaugh.
- To protect his public tough guy image.
- To have this judge elected to support his family's long-term wealth.

There you go, my assessment based on my limited knowledge. It is brief in order to summarize and provide speculation on my behalf. To expose in real time my bias, knowledge, opinions, and thoughts as this hearing ended.

I don't have all the details, or a crisp understanding of the true **motivation** of players and teams. That is how I would move forward. History should allow us to look back, to understand how the senate hearings and selection of Kavanaugh unfolded, and to learn about the full spectrum of **motivations**.

The selection of a Supreme Court Judge provided the opportunity to expand **GOM** to a complex human activity with limited personal expertise. I do this to expose the mechanics of the process that I use to define my personal position, beliefs, and opinions.

Finally, I will cover the legalization of marijuana for medical and recreational use, to lighten the mood. U.S. Senate hearings are important; however, the majority of us live life on a local level.

The Canadian Government passed legislation allowing the legal use of marijuana[8] on October 16, 2018. Bill C-45 the Cannabis Act[9] came into force on October 17, 2018. I do not want to dive into the operation of the government, as that is mundane and better covered by people with expert knowledge. The evidence that supports legalization is available. Risks, distribution and oversight have been defined. Are the details locked in and complete? No. These will be filled in as we move forward.

I covered **goal** and **organization** earlier, and want to focus on the **motivational** aspects.

The question is why has it taken so long to legalize marijuana. Maybe the industries that would become direct competitors utilized lobby tactics and emotional dogma to create fear. The alcohol and brewing industry may have created bias to show the bad side of the weed. This might protect them from another competitor and maintain their cash flow.

"Why did it take so long to legalize marijuana?"

Whether my speculation is true, is not the point.

My point is we need to clear the clutter to determine who is funding efforts to take public positions, and why they seek a specific outcome. We need to read the research literature and public papers and understand the authors' bias. We need to interview the authors and investigate their vested interest. Are research papers provided by independent research teams? Who funds the research teams directly and indirectly?

Why is the U.S. government sitting on the fence with legalization? Maybe private prisons need to be held at capacity in order to drive margins? Asking these kinds of questions provides a view that beckons.

We live in a time where major newspapers have been slapped with a fake news slogan. This new catchphrase is a slap down and a misleading con. Who do you trust? Where do you get your facts?

The problem is; who has the time to gather all the relevant information?

Why did I not dig into this topic 20 years ago? Fundamentally, my **motivation** back then was on raising a family and working like an addict to optimize cash flow.

The **goal** and the attributes of **oganizational** structure can be gathered, presented, and debated. The **motivation** of debaters has to be understood. It is the search and discovery of **motivational** logic that completes the picture and allows an intelligent, freethinking individual to make the best decision.

Free Speech Has A Price

Free speech has been a mantra for many societies. The assumption is that Free Speech is a right and in some cases the logic is documented into a legal framework for countries. In some societies, speaking out could cost a person their life. The utilization of the Internet, video and audio recorders have provided a means to make statements that can be captured forever. It is speculative as to the impact of a statement by any individual at any time. Terms can be used to move a nation, stimulate rebellion; resulting in a personal attack or injury to others. The ramifications of the statement may play into decisions, which impact our life; and we may never know how. Did your statement cost you a job? Who knows? The right to speak freely comes with an individual obligation to do so with truth. Truth by itself does not remove the risk tied to another perception of the truth.

—Brian R. Waldron

CHAPTER FOUR

GOM Evolution

There was a time I had GOD as my three-letter acronym. The letter "D" stood for Desire. I knew this was never going to be my final landing spot and a replacement word had to be found to dissuade religious bias.

The more constructive life is lived, the more positive life will be. Activities such as paying ideas forward, joining dots, solving problems, and sharing gifts and talents, provide positive feedback in ways you cannot predict. It takes time to allow dots to join before new adventures unfold.

This same logic must apply to negative feedback for common failings, job losses, illness such as cancer, and personal struggles. Tough times come to all of us, and without dwelling on my pain there are states of pain that have to be dealt with. Relief and knowledge will come from within and from experience. Most assurances will come from family and friends; others will come through community.

All feedback has to be processed and put into context to move forward. There are books on these topics, but first-hand experience defines you, to you.

In retrospect, being able to step forward is clouded in levels of doubt.

"First-hand experience defines you to you."

There are amazing stories about human survival, perseverance of handicapped people and struggles of minorities that highlight a significant theme. The **motivation** to survive, live, help, grow, strengthen and expand are core subjects to this common theme.

The word that felt correct was there all along; it took a personal struggle to have it jump out. My last epiphany came into focus, "**Motivation**" replaced "Desire" and **GOM** was established.

I had to grow beyond my youth. I tripped and fell, mended my ego, and moved forward. As I fought to rebuild myself, I found **GOM**. Here was a tool I could count on to help me.

I pissed people off. I learned how to use the back channels. I was fortunate to have great managers around me. I watched the best performers to gain experience in the art of dealing with people.

Was I a great manager? No. Was I good at providing feedback? Over time, I progressed.

I am not a person to tell anyone how to manage their business, unless they asked for my insight. In this, I would either be direct or play back my perceptions of their performance.

I did a review on a young engineer and stated I would not have hired him had I known more about his experiences. How low is that? The bad part is that is exactly what someone said to me, and I played it back to him projecting my failings onto him. I was disgusted with myself.

It took me years to rationalize this. I remember the room we were in and how upset he was. That crude statement may have been true, but my job was not to go into the past and whine. My job was to take what was happening with this young man, and between us help build our careers. I still owe him an apology.

My own engineering role carried employment risk within the **organization**. News that the company was going to evolve, and smaller operations would not survive, challenged me to accept an Engineering management position in a small factory operation of the Canadian Maritimes. Along with my young family, I took the risk and transferred to Amherst, Nova Scotia.

One attribute that helped me to get the job was growing up in a similar small town. The biggest concern was whether my family would be OK far away from our families. This was the first time in my life where the mental health of my family and me became a consideration.

Other families who transferred to the Amherst operation had difficulty integrating, or missed their families. This is not a criticism, but a realization. I had an inherent skill set that was considered part of the selection process. I was selected over managers that were more competent.

We loved living on the east coast. As with Kirkland Lake, people create their own environment as a place to be.

In another role of engineering management, my mentors warned me that my skill set did not match the needs and assertive nature of New Product Introduction. I took on this role as the business expanded into the wireless world. It was something I wanted to do. The art of introducing a new product covered a broad view of functional teams within a corporation.

It is odd looking back. I was the guy who was available verses the right guy. A safer route could have been taken. Why did I risk so much? What was my **motivation**?

The **motivational** details leading up to my decision are crisp, but only in retrospect. At the time, adventure, ego and learning were strong **motivators**. On the other hand, the "hunter" logic of my curiosity came into play.

What was beginning to formulate in my search for **GOM** was concern over events that initially did not make sense. In hindsight, when wisdom is gained, these events play into life's actions and become part of who I am.

The following attributes tied to work, life and experience, provided insight into my growth like pieces of a puzzle. Each is a story of learning and provided the bits and pieces of knowledge and wisdom to construct **GOM**. These are battles we go through to discover who we are.

Women and Men

My parents and family knew and respected the difference between men and women. It was never a thing of dominance.

I was taught as a guy to respect women in a way that required intellectual reasoning versus brute force. My male bias forced me to listen to women carefully to understand different perspectives. The process was never prescriptive or regimented. It was the way my parents saw things.

This environment influenced my teenage years. My introversion came across as weak or arrogant. I had girlfriends but only a few I dated. There are stories, which became life learning with bursts of humour, and embarrassing failures.

Entering the work world and having women as peers or bosses was intuitive and seen as equal competitors or mentors to men. When I listened to people working for me or around me, multiple viewpoints allowed me to make the best decisions. Decisions had to be managed to link directly to urgency. Typically, slower decisions were better. Slow decisions by any individual can be seen as weak. And at times I had to make little decisions till the best decision was exposed.

There is always the risk that the "right" decision can be wrong. It is all part of learning. My approach to this point is based on life as a teenager, influenced by family experience; input was equal between men and women. This felt natural.

Writing a Paper

I was selected to lead a paper submission to Canada Awards for Business Excellence[10]. The topic covered business and process improvements accomplished over previous years. The term "social engineering" was bantered about. To me, it was common sense and the art of behaving as mature adults. The ability of a team is defined by its capabilities and **motivation** to succeed.

The plant manager hauled me into his office one day and said he wanted someone more capable to do the paper. I knew he was right, but I was determined. I told him I would quit if we did not win. Walking out of that office, I cried. I had laid my job on the line and put my family at risk for ego. This was crushing. I told no one and worked my butt off.

I had no idea how to articulate a proper article, let alone sell the efforts of so many people. The opportunity to work with a great team and a good mentor helped craft the paper. The mentor was key to opening my eyes to see the depth of wisdom required to build teams.

We did not win. I prepared a letter of resignation and told my wife what I had done. She was not impressed. However, she was an optimist and said, "We will be okay."

I went to work and called the manager to state my position and offer my resignation. He asked what I had learned and then told me why we lost. It had nothing to do with me, and everything to do with the man who took over his Plant Manager role. He suggested I rip up my letter and move on. I did.

Science

There was one specific person who poked me in the right direction. She spoke her mind and managers struggled to deal with her. Eventually, she worked for me. What I discovered was an intelligent woman who had a huge heart and acted as a spokesperson for the quiet many. She sized me up quickly and worked her magic. She shifted me off the management dogma presented in books and provided simple science books instead. Her point was that the fundamental logic to work with people could be found in science.

As I read and she criticised, I began to understand. My thinking became more critical of a book's content and message. To verify truths, I needed the knowledge to pull out the best pieces of information. I discovered business management books took simple scientific data and extrapolated the facts into three hundred pages. Base points were valid but three hundred pages were extreme.

I read everything from management to current science theories. Specific science at the time included Chaos Theory[11] Systems Theory[12] and General Systems Theory.[12][13] Open systems was intriguing but many books were way beyond my analytical depth. The brief direct nature of the index provided context that intrigued me; I began to see patterns that tied to analytical layout of the chapters, and allowed me to focus on content that I wanted to explore.

It was while reading General Systems Theory[13] when **GOM** began to formulate. From my reading and work training, three phrases helped assess how a system worked at a high level. The three terms were: **goal**[14] **organization**[15] and **preservation of identity**.[16] Yes this is a over simplification of general systems theory, however these terms resonated with me. I started to use these phrases to test work environment and life in general.

On a business trip to the Canadian Maritimes I read "The 7 Habits of Highly Effective People"[17] by Steven Covey. It was then that I realized I could simplify his seven habits into my own memory jogger, **GOM**.

Team

Managers were constantly flooded with logic for promoting "the team." I get the logic of team. I grew up on winning and losing teams. I competed in sports, and played drums in a pipe band long enough to understand the concept of positional expertise. Instinctively, I knew that the positional expertise of individuals combines to create something greater than the simple sum of the parts. The idea of **1+1>=2** can define the success of the whole. How was it possible for groups to become teams and then to become successful? Failure in the struggle turned out to be the fastest means to learn.

$$1 + 1 > = 2$$

I observed the people who stepped out and took risks, started to shine. The gain was compounded for those who understood how to market their own actions. Doing something was better than waiting on a consensus. This apparent double standard took time to rationalize.

The team concept was also used to manage a member of our team. Anyone labelled a non-team player faced chastisement. It bothered me how the terms "leadership" and "team" became a form of verbal weaponry. In the worst-case managers were rebranded as members of the "leadership team". This implied that any manager was a leader. Leadership is one word of management vocabulary. To utilize the new brand belittles both management and leadership.

Keep it simple. Call a manager a manager, and a team a team. Any misuse of these terms is fodder for marketing clones.

GOM went a long way to create the vocabulary needed to construct teams. What is the **goal**? How to **organize** the right members? What is the **motivation**? For people I mentored that were to manage their own teams, I added a visual piece of data. I put my hand behind my head and raised five fingers, which was telling them to use their "radar" and listen. Then apply **GOM**.

Making Decisions

Being an engineer, a problem solver, and an introvert, I was seen as passive. The battle of clearing clutter or gathering information to make good decisions was an area to work on. At times I had the expertise to make the best decision. Most times the knowledge had to be gained. Decisions were made based on my ability to make "risk" calls. Finally, the light went on and I had an epiphany: There are times when a close decision is better than no decision. Sometimes no decision is the right decision.

There were people who took decision making to the extreme. They were a charm to watch, and I learned from their failings.

Humour

The utility of humour played a unique role as an icebreaker for job interviews. The hunt became how to find a humorous event that was familiar to the interviewer. Having interviewers laugh accomplished a positive start, and created a rapport that helped to take the edge off the interview. Humour didn't work all of the time and, when it failed, I knew something was amiss. Either my sense of humour was misaligned, or the interviewer was having a bad day, which raised a flag to investigate the work environment.

Competition

The greatest gift to the learning process is competition. It is built around success and failure. It comes with the rudimentary logic to force you to learn, whether you like it or not. The competitive nature of sports is a valid touchstone.

My dad was a military veteran who took part in the Second World War. War is a form of competition that promotes innovation. Yes, the innovations may be lethal weapons, jets, rockets, or submarines, all of which have peacetime applications. The war competition stimulates an environment where focus is crisp.

In college, I had peers who competed for marks. I worked harder and enjoyed the competition. At the end of the day, no one was addicted to false wishes of being smarter than anyone else. We were content with doing well and succeeding. The competition **motivated** us.

Experience is a Wonderful Teacher

The following historical events will detail how I refined my personal search to achieve the three-word acronym, **GOM**.

Graduating with a diploma in Civil Technology I migrated to Calgary to live during the oil boom. After a week of interviews, I had seven job offers on the table. Mission accomplished. Municipal engineering was the field I selected. The team I worked with would provide survey data needed to construct residential subdivisions around Calgary. The topography was dramatically different from the lakes and forests of Northern Ontario. Calgary is a city with visible mountains on the horizon and represented an adventure I had to take.

My attention span for any job was short at best. Challenges and learning were my drugs. Once a challenge was met or my learning slowed, it became time to move on. I was arrogant and aggressive.

The Calgary firm was taken over by a larger engineering company based out of Toronto and management quickly changed. I was integrated with PhDs, Scientists, and Engineers. Instantly, I was low in the ranks of educational status. This did not sit well with me and it stimulated an application and subsequent acceptance to Engineering school at the University of Calgary.

Within the first week of Electrical Engineering courses I panicked, this was out of my league. Full of fear, I considered transferring to Civil Engineering.

Refusing to quit, I made a beeline for the library and filled two backpacks with electrical engineering texts. Study began. My appointment with the Dean of Civil Engineering was never made and I graduated with a degree in Electrical Engineering.

The education I received was a true test of my abilities and vision. The challenge was refreshing and like a dream come true. It was an honour to graduate as a Canadian Engineer with an iconic Iron Ring[18]. There were bouts of arrogance after graduation but my true mentors put me in my place.

This new education stimulated a level of over-work. Workaholism is an insidious disease that engrained its teeth into my ethic. Thankfully, a good friend, who was a recovering alcoholic, pointed out the symptoms of addiction. Shocked, and in denial, it stuck in my brain and I fought to get my life back. Addiction is a battle of the mind that only one person can correct. It is about choosing to fix you first then moving on to give back or pay that knowledge forward.

Mentors

I have been blessed with great mentors from family to close friends, including young children who ask wonderful questions. I had work mentors who would push and challenge me, and often defeat me. Defeat is a positive term here as it forced exponential learning. My senior, wiser mentors seemed to see potential in people that others didn't have time to explore. The best mentors remain, others moved on. Over the years contact has been maintained with a few. Life moves forward.

Recently, I have searched out specific colleagues to thank them for mentorship they provided. They in turn provided background data surrounding information and events I was not privy to. Merging this new data into my chosen career path, exposed how "dots were joined" at the appropriate time.

"Mentors and Motivation provide mystical glue."

As a fresh engineer graduate, the latest business books on management fired me up. A wonderful mentor taught me to read critically to expose the greatness and weakness posed in the text. She suggested I consider the author and the author's beliefs. She pointed out how authors tend to integrate personal beliefs into their work. I was captured in shock and awe. This lady could probably read a four-hundred-page book in a couple of days. She carried brilliant skills and educational prowess. Why did she stop for me? She was one of the brilliant and patient people that helped me. Why was she so patient?

After graduation as an Electrical Engineer, my father in-law Ken became a naval officer in the Canadian Navy during the Second World War. During summer sessions away from school he worked in the mines of my hometown, Kirkland Lake. When mine managers discovered he was a baseball pitcher, he was assigned to surface work in order to protect him from danger and allowed him to focus on pitching for their team.

Ken taught me the basics of reading people, with live practice at airports.

This workshop was a true insight into the thinking of a man who had no fear and enjoyed meeting new people.

As an example, my family was travelling across Canada with a layover in Toronto. My in-laws joined us for the four-hour wait. Ken randomly selected a traveller and we each described the person.

Once we defined an individual we approached him, and Ken found a way to strike up a conversation with something as basic as, "Hello Bob, I haven't seen you in years." Of course, this wasn't Bob but Ken introduced himself with a guise to help them remember him. Within minutes, the individual would introduce themselves.

The scenario was inspirational. They traded business cards and guess what, he was eighty percent correct about "reading" his selected individual. With time and practice, I improved. An added bonus for me was overcoming my fear of talking to strangers.

Ken taught me about the oil and gas industry and the stock market. He loved science and the study of how the wealthy became wealthy. He studied world news and was on a more advanced search to mine. He was reading my science books and I was reading his science and business books. We had great conversations, although mostly one-way.

Ken was searching to find tangible links between historical biblical scriptures, faith, and science. I was searching for the best way to manage myself and my employees based on the science I was reading. I am thankful he was able to put more pieces of the puzzle together for me.

Religion in my mind was a business run by the church. The business model is one of collecting money for souls, using fear and ignorance to control its patrons. My cynical view took years to reshape with the help of a couple of friends. One was a young minister. Continued reading of physics and parallel sciences refocused my cynicism back into realism.

Upon graduation from university, my first job was as a production manager. I had thirty technologists and operators as subordinates. To this point, I had no special training in the art of managing people. It was a management task to communicate with my team weekly. On night shift, I gathered everyone together for a half-hour review. My boss and peers provided ideas regarding logistics and topics. Performance metrics were first, followed by business news then open the floor up to questions.

My intuition told me to explain a little about myself. Six words were defined on an overhead chart. Their source was built around my upbringing in Kirkland Lake, and experiences through university.

These words were carried forward as a reference to explain myself to any new team I would manage. They provided a way to break the ice and open myself up to questions about me, and how I managed myself, and others. They also provided a benchmark for team members to challenge me when I stepped outside my stated principles.

The list was:
- Freedom
- Honesty
- Respect
- Care
- Hunter
- Commitment

This list was intuitive and easy to create, however, remembering it was another story. A cheat sheet was required.

The "hunter" term was fun, as it usually created an expectation of aggression. As a teenager, I had been a hunter. One who relished the walk of exploration rather than the kill! I switched the gun for a camera and took long hikes through the bush, eager to know what was around that next corner.

The intriguing part was, managing people felt natural. No idea why, or if this was arrogant behaviour, but it felt right.

"I am a hunter with a loaded camera."

In my second year as a production manager, I had a young boss who was a guy to respect, yet he could be intimidating. He was a bully and he crushed my enthusiasm. Driven to meet or exceed targets and rise in the company he demanded control of every aspect. He had grown with the expansion of the local facilities and had a broad understanding of most aspects, but he did not have the capacity to do everything. He needed to learn to delegate, and to be a leader who allowed failure so that a person might grow.

As a rookie I wanted to succeed. Inadequate ratings were career limiting and emotionally challenging. I feared a poor rating in my annual review but managed to obtain "meet the standard." I was disappointed. My belief was that meeting a standard is mundane; exceeding was the way to go.

My manager did have a surprise for me, which he detested to tell me. He could not believe what employees, who worked for me, were telling him. Out comes his little yellow book of secrets and off he goes. The scenario was this: Someone on the team stated that, if I could part the Red Sea, they would plant grass and then bring me across in a chariot when all was well and the grass was blooming. This statement completely disrupted his logic on how to manage people. How in the world did a rookie get the majority of thirty people to become this loyal? I sat in shock. Is this good, or a disaster? I had to figure out what I was doing to receive such compliments in order to determine how to adapt.

The answer came when a young woman explained. She never took credit as the author although she knew details about the accolades. She said I treated people like people. When we worked overtime, I took on roles to fill in any gaps if we were not fully staffed. I listened, never judged, could relate to the conversation, was direct when needed, loved the humour and loud laughter on night shifts…the list went on.

In this **organization**, my perception was that these attributes were contrary to what my boss wanted. It took time to digest and find which path worked for me. Yes, this decision would define my future path within management ranks, and future roles in the corporation. CEO or any senior positions would never happen. I was upset and yet, I was happy with my decision to be me.

I remember the day a subordinate asked me the definition of quality. I rambled on with the jargon of the day. She smiled and answered, "It is a fair exchange." I sat back realizing how close she was. Quality teams within our structure would never appreciate such simple logic in place of their technical expertise on definitions and mathematics.

"Quality is a fair exchange."

That "fair exchange" phrase provided a path that opened up whole new areas of learning. It could be used to explain the selection of a hamburger, or locally purchased goods versus foreign goods, barter systems, and employee/employer relations. For example, I was hired to manage a team of people in exchange for a salary and benefits.

All along my thinking was naïve and immature. I viewed the managing world in which I worked as a political hornet's nest. Business politics had to be learned. It all came down to aggressive promotion of oneself and/or doing a great job. By default, and historical ethics, I chose the latter. Fundamentally, my humble upbringing seldom allowed self-promotion.

Business meetings were logical and effective communication tools utilized to gain a broad review, and define a plan to tackle **goals**. Reading meetings at face value and completing the tasks expected of each player created a learning environment to build interpersonal talents.

Great successes were wonderful and the majority of my endeavours were successful.

As my business acumen matured, it became apparent that the presentation of data and facts were biased. Now that is a nugget of rocket science intellect. In retrospect, it was meant to be this way in order for me to grow exponentially. It became a key task to understand the reason teams or individuals wanted to achieve a **goal**, as they were not always applying themselves for the same reasons. In a worst-case scenario, blind-side tactics took my breath away and put me in fear of losing my job.

I was blind-sided be negative events, which forced me to evaluate my personal understanding. How was it possible to be involved in a complex project assuming things are going well, when suddenly my boss appears and asks why the project is off the rails? What the ……?

It was obvious I needed a strategy to best assess my audience. The audience was competitive, assertive, intelligent, passionate, loyal, multi-cultural and **goal** driven. The tactic took years, plus a number of key events to reach a conclusion. The result was a memory tool that could be easily remembered and utilized in real time.

Goal, **Organization** and **Motivation** are the three words used as my memory tool to assess situations. This tactical crutch was utilized to understand the dynamics of business meetings, management groups, peers, individuals, and myself.

Poignant Point One

I struggled up a Tibetan mountain to find a monk sitting cross-legged on a flat stone. I asked the holy man what the secret to a long life was. He said, *"Keep breathing. Keep breathing."* I then said if I am to live a long life I need a **goal**. I must have a **goal**! The monk smiled at me and said, *"You do not need a* **goal** *in life, Life is the* **goal** *my son."*[19]

—Brian Walsh

CHAPTER FIVE

Goal

Everything has a **goal**.

The **goal** logic is part of our basic make up, a pre-programmed part of our Read Only Memory (ROM). It is fundamental to all things.

Humans have a unique intellectual ability to freely define **goals**. It is not that we are special, but unique in our ability to ascertain a **goal**. Humans have the strategic advantage to articulate **goals**. We can re-adjust a **goal**. We can reject a **goal**. We can freely define a **goal** to create a plan and accomplish that **goal**.

"Everything has a goal."

Physically, we cannot determine if inanimate objects have a **goal**. For example, does a rock have a **goal**? We cannot establish that a rock has a **goal**, but we instinctively know it has a purpose. This argument is based on common sense. If the purpose of a rock can be understood, I would say its purpose is its **goal**.

The acknowledgement that we have a limited ability to communicate with a rock allows me the ability to make basic assumptions on behalf of the rock. I suspect you are rubbing your head laughing, as "this guy is nuts" rolls through your brain. Is my arrogance clouding a topic with evidence of something you need no evidence for? Humour me and let me build my case.

"Does a rock have a goal or is it just a rock?"

To find the '**Goal**' as a significant attribute for **GOM** is a simple task. It is a matter of admitting this is true. To create the story, let me mix system theory and humour to explain.

The study of closed systems in thermodynamics at university was my first introduction to system logic. Closed systems consist of an environment that exchanges energy but does not exchange mass. The best example is the study of pressure vessels. Put water inside a vessel, seal and heat. With the proper tools, internal temperatures and corresponding pressures can be measured. This technology is used to heat homes and the human **goal** to keep warm in winter is achieved.

The idea of a closed system captured my attention, as did the concept of entropy.

This idea of entropy resonated often through my management world. The thought of decay over time, settling, and reducing to disorder is contrary to the learning process. You might say we lose entropy as we gain knowledge. In other words, we gain order as we learn, which is contrary to the mechanical systems we deal with. It became apparent to me, that humans may be self-programmed to **organize** chaos and becomes the base concept behind **goal**-driven robotics.

For years, scientists have explored chaos and string theories. One idea that inspired me was order in a natural process, which shows how chaotic chemistry can order itself. Reading "Order out of Chaos"[20] by Ilya Prigogine and Isabelle Stengers provided an understanding of chaos, and its relevance to chemistry. How does a chaotic system evolve into an ordered system? How does it know what form to take?

Closed systems and entropy were fundamental learning stages. Then along comes the big jump to the concept of open systems. Human beings, as individuals, are open systems living within an open system. Well, as open as we choose to be.

As observers, we can study ourselves, and our environment. In the study of most things, we take action and observe a result. The missing gap is, it took a thinking person to activate the experiment. What happens when I am the experiment and experimenter? Well, this bothered me. I acknowledge that my own bias may taint my **goal**. This may sound mundane, but it is intuitive and refreshing for me. I am an observer and actor with a known bias and I still move towards my **goal**. **Goals** are subjective and are implicitly biased. I am perfect with my flaws.

"I am perfect, so are my flaws."

To provide another metaphor to visualize the concept of perfect with flaws, I will link to statistics and the bell curves[21] of normal distribution. As individuals we fall on a normal distribution in terms of human construction, physically and mentally. The gross majority would fall in the heart of the curve. We are all different and yet similar. I use the term perfect verses normal, and the term flaw to define the variables that modify our being. Flaw is a direct way to state the contrary and act to balance the phrase. Each person is part of a normal distribution and perfect with the flaws. If the ego is in balance each person can discover who he or she is. There is need to manage the flaws. There is no need to be humble about you being you.

To shift metaphors and add humour let me provide an event that resonated in my life. I used jokes in presentations to act as a contrary position in times of stress, or to make a direct point. The power of a single joke provided an outlet for me to relax or create smiles within the audience.

I found a funny cartoon strip that stimulated a subtle idea. The joke itself is an inanimate object crafted on a page of a book. I looked at the joke, understanding the words and characters, I laughed. I mean, I laughed to the point of tears. Next time I read the joke I found it funny, but not hilarious. With this observation I started thinking about why.

What is the purpose of a joke? Was I overthinking? Yes, but this thought did happen.

The purpose is to make me laugh although the purpose may also be to make a direct or subtle point.

To demonstrate I offer a visual format to feature Poignant Point Two. View as a reflection of my opinion tied to a warped sense of humour.

Boydoc and Girldoc knew they were different and yet connected to the same source.

Poignant Point Two[22]

The balance between men and women is a powerful theme of our time. All things in nature require a balance, whether we want it or not. In this case, the artificial boy and girl can gather all the data and acknowledge similarities or differences. However, when there is a sudden imbalance, they realize they are dependent on a system. Unhooked from that system, they become broken. I utilize the software extension "doc" to parody higher education. My **goal** is to set a point in a bigger picture where we are unique members of a common system.

I played with the joke concept in order to see it is simply a visual and/or written form of communication. What is the **goal** of the author? I linked the joke to the **goal** mantra utilized throughout my working years.

My engineering work involved financial reviews, business plans, development of new products, process improvements, and employee reviews. Each had a defined **goal** and guidelines to work within. I saw them as tasks to be accomplished in exchange for wages.

The basic premise is that everything has a **goal**. Jokes, authors, employers, and chemical reactions all have **goals**.

Determining how a chemical reaction could have a **goal** is the tough part. Is it a form of biological or pre-defined intelligence or a state of equilibrium? Artificial intelligence is a term used to represent the concept of software, which collects data, **organized** in a constructive way to modify its own future actions. Are humans the next phase of a greater design collected into biological intelligence?

I explored all of these ideas and thought through each in terms of a **goal**. Closed mechanical systems are designed to accomplish tangible **goals**, such as heating a home. The universe is a state of entropy and will remain in that state until an external force acts on it. Will humans create a tangible butterfly effect, or black holes to act as an external force? At this time in my life, it is okay to settle with this logic. There is no need to drill deeper into chemical reactions. There are scientists working to determine deeper logic.

Another idea came after stepping on a beehive while cutting grass. My kids saw the event and laughed while I "danced like a crazy man". They had no idea I had been stung multiple times. Lucky for me the nest was small. I was pissed off and hurting. My lawn mower was stuck in the nest and I had to finish cutting the grass but I remember thinking, "why was the nest buried in my grass?"

For the next half hour my mind worked through the whole process to determine the beehive's **goal**? I laughed when I realized a beehive is an open system. I defined a set of **goals** for the hive. How it is structured physically, and by its population of queen, workers, and drones. The function of each bee is well defined and I did the follow up research.

It is this set of bee stings that locked in the term **goal** as a fundamental connection to all things. I went on to challenge everyone to define anything that did not have a **goal**, or purpose. Well, at least until everyone got bored of my pestering and walked away.

> *"A set of bee stings locked in the term goal as a fundamental piece to all things."*

Poignant Point Three

*"Good **organization** is like being fluent in a second language. Bad **organization**— only knowing the swear words."*[23]
—Mark Kossek

CHAPTER SIX
Organization

Organization is a broad topic. The mechanical and structural items necessary to complete the **goal**, includes physical and emotional attributes. Physical attributes are **organizational** structure within a business or government; tools needed to produce a product; structures needed to house people or employees; educational expertise and defined boundary rules. Emotional attributes can include teaming, winning, losing, capabilities, or love.

Emotional attributes take effort to delineate **organizational** and/or **motivational** linkages. An example is the love between people. The **motivational** aspect of love may result in the birth of a child. It can also be part of an **organizational** make up. Do people of any defined group have an affection that creates a form of glue that binds them together?

Over time I learned that **Organization** contains all attributes that do not fit under **Goal** and **Motivation**. Attributes I associate with **Organization** are physical and/or intellectual in nature. At the end of the day, I did not require rocket science precision. Close was good.

"Living does not require rocket science precision."

I rely on science as the best knowledge base we have. Is it always correct? That is a valid question. It progresses with new knowledge, builds on what is available, and can be used for good and/or evil. Scientific research proves or disproves theories. One attribute I respect about great scientists is, they understand they have a brief moment in time to add nuggets of knowledge to society.

I look to scientific data to validate or disprove my own logic and bias. I have faith that scientific communities will progress to overcome the politics of the day.

A book on General Systems Theory[24] proves concepts explicitly in terms of **Goal** and **Organization**. This finding solidified my belief that the term **Organization** is key to developing a simple acronym.

Albert Einstein, in all his behaviours, was a man I respect. I cannot say I agree with all that he did in his life. Neither can I judge him fairly via textbook reviews. I could never live in his shoes; but I have to be able to understand him, his relationships and his science. Books on Einstein [25][26][27] opened up concepts that translated into layman language. It was in metaphors, and linkage to human experience where his work shone through and I understood it.

A number of scientists have carried on Einstein's work and they do a beautiful job of communicating in a language I understand. One example would be American Physicist, Dr. Michio Kaku[28] co-founder of String Field Theory, who is said to carry on Einstein's *"quest to unite the four fundamental forces of nature into a single grand unified theory of everything."* [29] Dr. Kaku has a number of books and on-line video clips. The video clips provide layman level insight into complex topics. Kaku is a physicist that provides a link to faith and science.

What I found frustrating in my science reading was I did not have the technical depth to fully understand and validate the mathematics, physics, biology, psychology, or the link to religion. There are people who will validate or disprove detailed science and mathematics, knowing this I moved forward. I discovered I could glean logic when metaphors are properly understood.

I get passionate about the linkage between public events and science. Few people are interested in debates that will push their beliefs to the edge with rational arguments. Fewer who get into great discussions, have like-minded thinking, or are contrary on specific topics. It is contrary opinion that pushes me and it is refreshing, especially when knowledge supports argument. Sometimes, I give a win in terms of argument and then do my own research. Most times, I garner a new nugget of useful data or information.

One of the best analogies I have used to describe learning for a person is an operational amplifier[30]. I was an electrical engineering undergraduate when the transistor was the rage. Transistors are the key electronic component to construct an operational amplifier. The common application was my stereo. One op-amp configuration is depicted here.

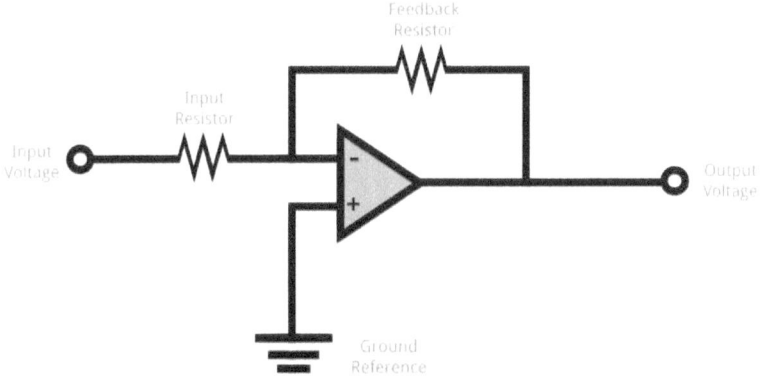

Electronic circuit symbol for an operational amplifier[31]

The triangle symbol represents the electronics needed to function as an amplifier; on the left inputs are noted as "-" and "+". Output is the prescriptive yield needed to support the environment it is designed into. The feedback loop is provided through a resistor. Feedback is needed to adapt the input required to ensure the output is meeting its design intent. Adding software creates a form of "artificial intelligence."

My electronic metaphor describes symbolically how an individual or a team of people operates and learns. As humans absorb input, we act in a way that creates wanted output, and study the feedback to adjust as needed. This is a visual model based on a symbol of complex electronics, which has followed me through my career.

> *"Scientific communities overcome the politics of the day."*

Let me create a list of attributes that fit under the **organization** umbrella. It is a broad list narrowed in scope to deal with the obvious, and maybe not so obvious. I will work from big to small and end with my own world of new product introduction. I do this to make my points relative, because everything is relative. Relevance is the objective of any attribute or situation.

I want to cover a broad scope offering a multitude of examples versus one metaphor, which will define a life, lived. These specific attributes grew over my life and allowed me to "see" how they fit under **organization**. I open up the logic to include speculation and ideas that I wonder about.

I will state my logic or ask questions to gain the view of **organization** or structure for each attribute. The question framework offers an open-ended thought to challenge my own thinking. I do this to let you know that I am one person with thoughts beyond academia.

The list is long and it may be confrontational or contrary to your logic.

The Universe

It is structured with galaxies, stars, planets, black holes, life and time. We speculate and research how the universe was created. The prediction of our universal future is then based on historic evidence.

Nature

The rock we walk on. The food we eat. It consists of the scientific make up of all physical earthly things, some of which are: trees, bees, water, gold, air, and humans. All life "farms" the earth resources and adapts into the environment. Is there a structure in which nature is above or below human rank and order? Is nature subservient to the human? How does nature play into business decisions? How does nature play into our decisions on products we buy or sell?

Humans

Wow! The current form of biological intelligence is a phenomenal machine. This delicate biological form has a physical and mental make-up that provides a strategic advantage over other forms of nature. Assuming humans are all important leads to unbalance. We are integrated with nature, not master of nature. A single human is structured to effect tasks. Binary humans are designed to propagate and raise children. As a team, various skills are combined to construct physical objects, to farm in communities, to share relationships, to communicate and to learn.

Was this human machine created by chance? Are we alone? How and why do we **organize** into groups? Do we have five senses or more? Are we followers, leaders, or both? How do we communicate? How do we adapt? What do we adapt to? Are humans manipulated by money to bias opinion and action?

Gender

I thought I would split this one off to stand-alone. There are two major genders (in general). There are other non-binary genders, which I respect. To simplify I focus on binary logic and what I know, women and men. How these two sexes progress or adapt is a study unto itself.

The basic structure of a human is dictated by gender. We are physically different, and I would argue "wired" differently, and as such **organized** in ways that compliment each other. Physical biology and wiring have a basic make up, pre-programmed long before birth. I believe it is broader than binary. Concepts of reversal therapy were used in cruel and fraught attempts to modify a person through physical and/or mental adaption. Adapting could also come from abuse, peers, community, belief systems, education or forms of dogma.

Race

Various races on the planet are variants of the base human machine at different stages of evolution, living in cities, or jungles untouched by modernity. They are influenced by history and environment in terms of knowledge, physical climate, and resources.

Is one race better than another? I think not. Does any race or group grow to understand how to use power and fear to dominate? History has exposed our inability to accept the varieties of races in a holistic way. We are still in an immature point of evolution. Maybe the maturity is designed as a predefined weakness that forces each person and generation to learn. Maybe the friction between races is there to teach us.

To profile a person or group is a term used to create a physical and mental framework of **organizational** logic. Profiling can be used to understand a person, a group, or their behaviour. What is the bias in the profile? What is the bias in the profile creator? Basic science logic plays in here with the ability of the observer to objectively observe. Or is the act of observation, part of the profile?

Animal Kingdom

I would argue all forms of animals are machine variants evolved to operate within a system. The sum of the whole creates balance in the overall environment. Energy can be closed, added and removed, but mass is never added or removed. Mass balances out with movement between earthly things. If we disturb the balance, do we disturb the mass?

What evidence do we need to create a physical plan to maintain nature's balance in the animal kingdom? Will nature take care of the balance? Nature itself will survive; will humans? Do we need earth-threatening events to stimulate holistic global approaches? The interesting aspect about this debate is, until the future arrives, we will not know how decisions made today will play out.

Education

This includes educational structures and belief systems used to propagate data and knowledge. Which university degree do you possess? Does this degree have value? Is this education used to create or define a robot for a factory? What education is needed to be in the military, to be a first responder, to work with machines or to manage people? What education is required for a job interview? How do we define brain washing versus education?

Understanding the education of an individual plays a critical part in understanding their behaviour and actions, individually or within an **organization**.

Capabilities: Physical and Mental. Learning Abilities

I lump these together as they are tied together. The capabilities of individuals and teams are the key make up of human based **organizations**.

Machines have a set of capabilities. There are those in society who will argue we are pushing artificial intelligence to the point where machines can make decisions and react faster than humans.

The concept of artificial intelligence intrigues me. Are humans analog systems, designed in an advanced lab? My assumption is we are not created by random events. This assumption opens up a whole spectrum of research and thinking. Are we biological intelligence models created by a society, which ventured through a digital version of artificial intelligence a million years ago?

> *"Are we biological intelligence models?"*

This thinking is now intuitive and yet one could argue there might be a loose connection in my wiring. I live in a society with data at my fingertips. I have to figure out what is good information. The capability to sort good information is directly linked to my mental capability and my ability to learn.

Science and Scientific Methods

Through time, humans push boundaries and discover new knowledge. This knowledge has to be supported or debated to ensure relevance and applicability. It is never free. It takes investment of time and resources. The products resulting from scientific research are the most succinct examples of societies who are **organized** to utilize technology.

The equation E=mc² [32] defined by Albert Einstein states that mass is energy. What a profound statement. Have you sat around a campfire watching a log burn? The energy of the fire and light are the results of the conversion of the log mass. Today, science continues to evaluate many of the historic science positions to constantly define relevance.

What science-based logic supports the engineering of your life? Do you use a cell phone? Can you communicate to people on the other side of the world? Do you wear a wedding ring? Do you drive a car?

I cannot see the future. I have to make my opinions and decisions based on the scientific data I have.

Complexity

I use complexity as an **organizational** piece because it defines the challenge to discover. As curious creatures, we see complexity as a measure based on the knowledge we comprehend. How complex is it to drive a car? Is the topic of physics complex? Is the concept of addition complex? How complex is the product to be developed?

I discovered a formula that numerically defines how complex it is to manage a team of people.

- **C = 2** to the power of **n**, where **n** equals the number of people on the team.

$$C = 2^n$$

In later years, when I worked with teams of multiple languages, I re-defined the complexity equation.

- **C = 2** to the power of **n + l**, where **n** equals the number of team members, and **l** equals the number of languages.

$$C = 2^{(n+l)}$$

Governing Entities

A natural process for humans is the ability to gather into common groups. As the group grows there is a need to **organize** to survive or build. A structural piece of this **organization** is the art of leadership. Each member can be a leader of his or her sub set within society. In order to tackle larger broader tasks for the group, a management structure evolves to oversee effective utility of resources. This is natural and efficient. Governments are an example. How did they evolve over time? How do they add value? How do they physically work? For example, how do I obtain a driver's licence? What is a government's bias? What are their strengths and weaknesses?

Religion

Religion is an example of an **organization** that is bound by a common belief. We see the physical structures such as church building, followers, leaders, financial models, and relevant books. There is published belief logic, and interpretation or misinterpretation of historic data. What are congregational behavioural patterns and bias? What is its linkage to science? How does religion influence a person's beliefs and actions?

Commercial and Industrial Entities

Business entities are **organizations** created to provide products or services. Business structures, **goals**, revenues, technology, spending, ethics, bias, all have to be understood in order to define relevance within the entity. This is where I worked to gain an income as a fair exchange for my services. I had to trade off job prospects with my own fears and capabilities.

War and Peace

War requires disciplined members within military **organizations** in order to defend or defeat an opponent. Peace requires a level of cooperation between warring parties.

Cooperation is the constructive word here. It may be forced cooperation or death.

War appears to follow the logic of entropy with a twist. There is a winner and a loser. The winner has a choice of how they deal with the loser. The winner can build or propagate an unnatural chaos. Peace requires documented agreements, verbal or symbiotic, to resolve chaos. It is my belief that we are programmed to grow and build in entropy. Are we mature enough to do this for all people on earth?

Power

Power is a word that can glue a society together. Power within an **organization** may represent a significant brand or the intellectual and physical strength of an individual to assert their wants on others.

The word "power" has a number of meanings. Is it the power to light a building. or the power to drive humans in a certain direction? Structures required to convert energy into electrical power are well documented.

The concept of human power takes significant knowledge and experience. Why is one person powerful? How does wealth play into this? What position do they hold: manager, director, captain, general, or priest? What is their credibility, expertise, knowledge, or bias? How do they project themselves? How do they dress? What physical position do they take in an office meeting, head of table or side of table? What is their body language?

Money or Currency

Currency is a measure used to define an exchange value. It provides a mechanism to barter among individuals or groups. What is the source of money? Is there enough? Can you convert risk to financial terms? Are we working within a barter system? What is the worth of the various currencies around the world?

What is the value of time? Can I spend more to do something faster or better? Does MacDonald's make the best hamburger or the most economical burger in terms of a dollar paid? Is money the tool or the **motivator**?

Competition

War is an extreme form of competition. Competition itself allows an individual or group to maximize focus on specific **goals**. The friction created among competitors builds the knowledge needed to move forward, to win, to excel and to learn. Is this a hockey game? Is this war? Is this a competition between products, belief systems, facts, or the best utilization of resources? Competition is a trait that has to be managed in order to focus on legitimate **goals**. **Motivational** issues do play a role with competition and may or may not be obvious.

Bias

We have to understand the bias of any individual or group to understand their tactics and actions. This is true for any individual or **organization**. I thank my grandmother and a Grade 10 science teacher for an introduction to bias at a young age.

As a teenager, I was explaining an article in the local newspaper, when my grandmother challenged my understanding. It was not that she told me I was wrong. She suggested I had to understand who wrote the article and why they had a purpose to present the data in a unique way. My grandmother had been part of the event and knew exactly what the truth was. She explained the truth to me and asked what the difference was between what she presented and the author's version. Well, it turns out he had left out key pieces of information and created a story to favour his opinion, and the opinion of his **organization**. My grandmother exposed the bias to me.

In Grade 10 a science teacher asked the class to write a paper to prove the moon landing had actually happened. I remember the laughter of my classmates as we went away and wrote our papers. We found volumes of pictures, copied quotes from various sources, and submitted our reports. The teacher asked us how any of this material proved man landed on the moon, versus using a desert movie set.

I remember trying not to laugh at such a stupid idea. Then she explained. The only person that will know if man walked on the moon is the person who was there. The rest of us assume the data is reliable. Wow, what a concept for a student in Grade 10 to realize. This teacher provided me with the right to challenge anything, and to dig in and gather the best data available to support my decision and beliefs.

Love

Okay, let me play with an emotion. Can you measure love? Does love have different meanings? Does love grow or shrink? Do animals love each other? Does a tree love earth and water or a dog peeing on its trunk?

There are metrics that can be used to measure love. I can put a scale together ranging through contempt, hate, dislike; neutral, like, and infatuation. I use it here to show a structural logic to assess a situation tied to love. Do I "like" the team I work with? Do I "hate" the team I work with?

> *"Does a tree love a dog peeing on its trunk?"*

Beliefs

To understand the profile of an individual or team I have to understand their beliefs. Beliefs create a pattern that influences behaviour and how actions are **organized**. What religion has influenced an individual? What education has been gained? How did their upbringing influence their behaviour? What generation are they part of? What is their age?

For a team, what is the mix of beliefs within the group? How do they communicate? What do they communicate?

Rocks

I talked earlier about a rock and its **goal** or purpose. How does **organization** fit with a rock? There is molecular makeup to create minerals and rock structure. Science has created models of how molecular pieces fit together, and interact. Add more rocks and lava and you get a big rock called planet earth.

Molecular Science

How small is small? Is our ability to study small things, limited by the tools at our disposal? Is there a limit to small, or is it an extension of the universe seen through special tools? Does small continue to infinity? Is the universe infinite? What does infinite mean?

Understanding how the tiny is **organized** provides a view of how the pieces add up to the whole or pieces of the whole.

Honey Bees

The structure of a bee colony is a wonderful metaphor. There is the nest; the hierarchy of bees within the hive; the physical environment, weather, predators, and resources such as pollen. Each member has a pre-programmed logic used to fulfill a purpose as an integral part of the hive. Each bee is built within the hive. They forage for food and in their travels move pollen from plant to plant. The honeybee is an integral part of nature and plays a role in its balance.

What is the **goal** of a honeybee? I would propose it to be the propagation and pollination of flowers. Honey would be the product manufactured to feed the colony. What is their **motivation**? Could it be continuance? Over-simplified, yes, but that is what resonated with me.

Bees live a life cycle adapted to their environment. Can they define a **goal** that says they will no longer make honey? I think not. The ability to define a unique **goal** outside a predefined scope happens as nature adjusts the environment and the behaviour of bees.

This list of attributes fits under the **organization** umbrella. They provide piecemeal examples on a number of topics. Specific attributes played a significant role in my evolution and were explored in detail during my tenure introducing new products. I will use my work world as an example, to show how my thinking is relative to the physical world of New Product Introduction.

Living World Summary for New Product Introduction

I spent my working life introducing new products. Functional experts were provided to teams in order to cover various aspects needed to develop, build, deliver, sell, and support products. It was a field documented by the art of engineering and project management. Project management was used for building pyramids, sailing ships, rockets, phones, and computers. I am not beholden to the world of project management; I simply recognized a logical method to **organize** and breed success.

A New Product Engineering management job came to me at a time when the business was expanding faster than we could ever provide expert people to support it. A dream job allowed me to discover all functions of business. This was a massive **organization** and my knowledge of other functional areas was simplistic at best. As an operations guy I had zero experience in development. I understood assembly, test, and configuration of mainframe telecommunication equipment.

The team members were spread across North America and around the world. I understood **goals**, structures, players, capabilities, risks, and budgets. We communicated via phone, email, team reviews, and regular project reviews.

This job was going to be a learning experience of trial by fire, as I lacked the appropriate experience. It took broader knowledge to understand workplace politics. What I had to learn was how to manage expectations across North America and within my local teams.

Over the next couple of years, I hired and **organized** a team of twenty project managers. This was a journey saved by mentors and spies. My interest was in understanding why teams were either successful or they failed. I wanted to know what was needed to make a team blossom and succeed, even when the risk was extreme.

Goal:

The **goal** was to develop and deliver a new product by a fixed time. Metrics were utilized to measure sub **goals** tied to functionality, timing, revenues, costs and delivery. The best measure of success was in positive financial payback.

Organization:

Structures were defined and resource technologies were collected to support the new product. Capabilities had to be exposed, especially on the technology side. Did we have the technology to complete the design? Did we have the capacity to deliver the right product as defined by customers willing to pay?

A new product introduction procedure employing a staged gate process provided a framework to manage. At a rudimentary level, we used critical path methodologies, utilized within the field of Civil Engineering. People can adapt and react to issues causing delays or unexpected risks. Was it perfect? No. Was it close? Yes. Was close good enough? Yes.

There were project teams defined with members of each functional team involved. The overall project team included development, marketing, field teams, finance, and operations along with a multitude of sub teams that managed each functional area.

Two examples are manufacturing and supply teams.

Manufacturing teams designed and assembled the required equipment to support the projected steady-state capacity. Supply teams managed suppliers, tooling capital for plastics, metal works, new chip sets, and other materials associated with the product part list.

Prototypes were built at each stage of development and stressed to ensure they met design intent. Well-trained people worked through the "bugs." We installed factory capacity in stages to support low volume prototypes, and scaled the increase to match projected deliveries. Material supply lines were established to match factory capacity.

On-line global software was built to integrate the project management process with the new product introduction process. The effort to maintain data drew on resources needed to do the physical work and at times created self-imposed administration delays. It could be managed to define any individual team's want, but cross-country teams could not validate the accuracy of the data. The software did provide a "big brother" tool, which drove additional effort to fully explain details that observers could not understand. At the time, computer dependency out-weighed the need for human intellect and the ability to negotiate.

In the end, the computer dependency was determined to be counter-productive. Base time-lines were managed at a global level with major milestones. Details were the responsibility of each functional team. We went back to human leadership and basic software tools.

I was naïve to the art of new product introduction within a structured company. I will use two specific examples to describe how lucky I was. I integrate **organization** topics and **motivational** issues in order to complete the New Product Introduction metaphor.

Example 1:

A team on the other side of the country was designing one of our products. One day our local project manager walked into my office to review a venture that was in trouble. This was happening in preparation for a project review the next day. He assessed the technical aspects of our deliverables in 10 minutes and spent 5 minutes explaining what was wrong. He spent the next 45 minutes explaining the mode of operation for the specific design team.

Explaining the behaviours of the team and their manager, he defined who was capable and trustworthy and who was not. The design manager was not trust worthy. As financial bonuses were tied to the team's deliverables, the design manager believed offence was the best defence in times of trouble. When there were technical issues the design manager did not want to expose, he would find a way to direct attention onto other people's work. This became known as the "smoke and mirrors" or "grenade launch" approach.

The local project manager coached me to act as the ultimate authority for our team; to act as the person who was the top manager on our site. This was not true, but it provided leverage to manage the rogue design manager.

This specific manager lambasted team members in public for failings of different kinds. Our team prepared each time, knowing what the issue was and that development members needed time to correct a bug. It was my objective to take the heat, as long as we could support the project overall.

Did we make mistakes during the development of a product? Yes, and we owned up to our errors in public, preparing our management structure in case there was a challenge through back channels. It was better to prepare the boss of a pending "big" issue.

My mentor's insight allowed me to gain credibility with the development team. I ran management smoke and mirrors to act as an authority figure.

A number of years later, I met the design manager. He discovered I had a boss he could have used to manage me. After I filled my boss in on the design manager's mode of management, I was glad to hand him off. That design manager was later fired. I never did find out why. I didn't care. A design member I knew and respected replaced him.

Example 2:

For this example, I offer a performance review and the art of making decisions. In the new product manager role, it was better to make reasonable decisions and take a risk than to sit idle. This became apparent during the annual review of our company when we were growing and hiring hundreds of people.

I prepared the details for my performance review into three binders of evidentiary material to show that I had accomplished the objectives. Work had been so busy I seldom talked to my boss or his boss. I worked in isolation and had grown into the role. In the office with my bosses, I sat at a round table looking out the window thinking I could be outside in a few minutes.

To my surprise, I was not asked to speak. My boss had details of the objective measures, and he told me about me, and my performance. He told me about the performance of my overall team, and our ability to **organize** within chaos to move everything forward. Yes, there were failures. One product was cancelled and we held the corresponding inventory. Turns out I could not be held accountable because of a failure elsewhere. I exceeded that year and received my bonus. I walked out of that office floating on air.

I gained a whole new level of knowledge and wisdom that day and I could feel it.

My New Product Introduction experiences provided hard physical, and mental training. The recipe needed to manage in a world of complex people relationships. It solidified the term **Goal** and **Organization** as key pillars for my acronym **GOM**. The experience introduced me to **motivational** events that shook me to the core. I needed to figure out how workplace politics played into **GOM**. Some were obvious. Most were not.

"Close is good enough."

Poignant Point Four

*"**Motivation** is a lot like love, not necessarily logical, always inspirational."*[33]

—Mark Kossek

CHAPTER SEVEN
Motivation

August 7, 2020.

Vacationing at a cottage on a beautiful lake near Mont Tremblant, Quebec, I sat looking out over the water to reflect on the times. I had been out for a kayak ride to refresh and clear my mind.

Motivation is the spirit of drive. **Motivation** will instil energy into the effort to **organize** and accomplish the **goal**. **Motivation** can range from self or group control, to a fundamental piece of the human psyche. **Motivation** is the emotional or intuitive member of the acronym.

Motivation tends to be the most mysterious to determine. It is not always apparent why things happen as they do. Why did the legalization of marijuana take so long? Why has gambling become so freely available? Why does my boss react in a certain way? Why do my friends like me?

The Coronavirus captured the focus of the world, displaying three major global realities. **First** is the rapid viral effect of Internet communication. **Second** is clear delineation in the definition of government leadership and non-leadership. **Third** is the task of dealing with a lack of protection for the most vulnerable and front-line responders.

The third item could be a delayed reaction as we work to determine the path and impacts of the virus. The medical statistics have provided a reasonable level of accuracy. Until we design and validate a vaccine, all are at risk, some more than others. It is my belief from this day forward that all vulnerable people in developed nations will be protected.

The viral effect of Internet communications, linked to precise examples of the lack of top-level leadership, has created a set of confused countries. The management logic is simple. Central governments need to define an overall plan, manage rare resources such as personal protective equipment (PPE), utilize the best medical experts, and analyse consistent statistical data. Local governments would then customize plans to regions, provide centralized communication to the public, implement tactical plans, and collect consistent data. Communication channels could provide real data and associated uncertainty. Most adults are mature enough to understand that precision is not available.

When a head of state capitulates to unproven theories, they spark an Internet viral response. The reaction is a human response aiming to obtain the best logic to help themselves and their neighbours. However, under the guise of freedom of speech, a manipulative marketing game can be played in order to bias a set of views and specific revenue streams. In the case of the U.S. President, I want to know the **motivation** that was driving him and his actions during this pandemic period. I can assume potential **motivations**, and that is the damning point.

Any one person can assume a theory and propagate data via the Internet. However, when a President propagates his belief, people listen. If that message is misguided or wrong, the impact is catastrophic for both him, and the population as a whole.

How do I determine a way to measure or trust the President? I feel like a child who wants to learn to blow bubbles with gum. Some children are taught how to blow bubbles, others learn bubble blowing on their own, some never learn to blow bubbles while others get gum in their hair. With this President, you are on your own. Can you find a way to make a President laugh about getting gum stuck in his hair and then capture your own ten seconds of global attention? Can you say Internet?

How did I come up with **Motivation** as the third pillar of my **GOM**?

I toyed with the word Desire. It had a sense of greed, like a child taking a treasured toy from another kid. Desire was momentary and I knew the acronym GOD would meet with predisposed bias. I did not want to bias anyone. I needed my words to be generic.

I am confidant my **motivation** arose out of working with new product introductions, driven by the underlying nontechnical stuff that defines how we think. The work-teams and bad actors exposed the term **motivation** through their behaviours. It was in these behaviours I was forced to figure out what was happening.

The repeated question "why" drills into layers of **motivation**. I discovered a repeatable pattern with the questions I was asking: *"Why did this happen?"* followed by *"What was the motivation that drove this individual?"*

Motivation had broader implications and was a mystery to determine. When combined with public stories around survival and perseverance for a variety of people, the term resonates to the top. It has an emotional link. It provides a forward and backwards looking span.

I continued to perform **GOM** stress tests. It worked and I could easily categorize physical and mental attributes under the three headings. Was it perfect? No. I needed "close." Close was good enough. As I used to say, "Perfect, with a margin of error."

"GOM was "perfect" with a margin of error."

I am asking why the President of the United States lies? Is he too stupid to know better? Is incorrect information being provided to him? Is he driven by something deeper, and lying becomes a projection of his true personal belief about himself? Add money to a pathological liar and he grows to believe his own lies. He has always lied and that is all he knows. He is an expert at denial.

I am no psychologist, but I know constantly lying is not right. My sense is he believes his weaknesses will be exposed if his ego is touched. His false front of lying keeps him isolated unto himself.

Something is wrong with that man. I do not trust him. It is like a bad accident, where you cannot help but look.

I have written about **organizational** attributes, now I will add **motivational** linkages to complete the logic with questions or statements around topics from the previous chapter.

War and Peace

Behind all wars is tangible evidence about their causes documented in history books. It is one thing to want to defend yourself and a totally different aspect to want to conquer. There is always a theme that drives the aggression to conquer. It can be as simple as a deflated ego or the wish for possessions. Peace requires an intellectual desire to cooperate or dominate. The energy that drives peace may result from the defeat of the aggressor, the recognition of waste or the exhaustion of resources.

Why have wars been fought? What triggers war? What is the **motivation**? Is it the need for food, water, wealth, or ego? Power and wealth are themes that often drive wars. Is the equivalent of war a burning forest, which creates a rebirth of the forest? Is peace the "end result" of war or the beginning phase of **re-organization**?

What would be the emotional make up of a person who will die for honour, or kill others because of their beliefs? How does ego play into the **motivation**? How do military powers convince a soldier to fight to the death?

Are people on the planet like all other forms of nature? Nature has evolved over time and we see the extinction of many species, so why would humans be any different? Are humans wired to cooperate or are guidelines required to keep society civil? Is cooperation the ultimate test as a planet?

Are we an experiment of a greater society searching for peace or ways to manage themselves?

Religion

Religion is one of the oldest business enterprises on the planet. Is the religious perspective of a greater being, the basis for a pattern of behaviours creating hierarchies of people? Assuming the greater being is at the top, does this drive the want to be at the top? Assuming the greater being is more powerful, does this create an image of good or bad? How has the structural bias been used to **motivate** a follower to follow? Is morality and education the **motivation**? Is financial wealth and power the **motivation**?

Religions cover the basics, in terms of faith and a like-minded community. It starts as a group to benefit the whole, and then evolves to the continuance of one's team. Throw rocks at my house and I will build a wall with the rocks. Management of a global enterprise will not happen on wishes and beliefs. Management happens via **organizational** structure driven by a set of **goals**. **Organization** has crafted logic to enhance or addict an individual's **motivation** to support the enterprise.

> *"Religion can hoard bodies and minds.*
> *Do we build walls with the rocks*
> *thrown at our camp?"*

How does religion influence a person's thinking? How can a person be managed into a belief system where they freely give up their earnings, body, and soul? I believe this archaic model is integrated into groups and businesses. Behavioural scientists can provide deeper thinking.

My point is, I think about these things and I have to define for myself, what I will believe.

Gender

Why are there two basic genders? Are there other genders? To keep it simple, I will deal with the two genders I am familiar with. What **motivates** a boy to like a girl and vice versa? Do you remember when you started to take notice of the opposite or same sex, as more than a person to ride bikes with? What was it that told you they would be of interest?

Are we pre-programmed to appreciate the opposite or same sex as we mature? How does nature handle the differences in sexes? Do the majority of nature's species need partners to propagate? Is the basic **motivation** the continuance of the species? Is sex the **motivation**?

As I grew up there was little rationalisation of how I began to like girls. I had parents and grandparents who presented a model of how the man and woman joined to create a family.

I compare these ideas to other living beings, such as the honeybee population. The bee colony has a single queen to propagate the members. The drone on first appearance does not fit the make-up of the hive. I assume they have no purpose, which confused me, until I do the research. I needed to learn their sexual role, to know that they are part of thriving hives in some percentage.

I have family members who are not attracted to the opposite sex. Early in my life I did not understand this. I discovered through further research the difference is natural. I grew to not judge others, who do not aspire to my make-up and beliefs.

Why did this matter to me? Sometimes we understand things in certain ways. What may appear obvious is not always obvious. I had to dig deeper to find positive understanding.

It is easier to gather tangible details or symptoms than to determine why people are **motivated**. The solution is taking time and energy, and a good selection of sources to gather accurate facts. Digging deeper may expose things I did not want to know, or it might go against my belief systems. Delving into **motivational** factors is hard work and likely to expose only a percentage of the truth.

I used the logic of "taking a position" in heated debates during business meetings. It helps relieve the pressure allowing me to state a defined position with hopes of having opponents open up their bias or **motivations**. I take a position and work to ensure it is valid. My ego and bias have to be managed in order to remain open to new ideas.

You have to use statistical logic tied to uncertainty to make your own decisions. The mathematics is a metaphor as we process the decisions with little mathematics.

*"Take a position. Let others challenge your position. Sit back and watch bias and **motivation** unfold."*

Following I have two examples of how **motivational** logic adds to the decisions I make.

Let me reflect back to my personal analysis of the Senate hearings to determine the selection of Judge Brett Kavanaugh. As of Saturday October 6, 2018, Kavanaugh has been confirmed to the Supreme Court of the USA. Kavanaugh's selection casts a data point on the U.S. global leadership decline. The Democratic primary win shifted power and made a lame President, a lame duck.

Over the history of the world, brief burst of societal wisdom and grace are found. The era of this U.S. President is far from graceful, or intellectual.

Based on the behaviour of the President of the United States and his subsequent belittling of Dr. Christine Blasey Ford, it appears women are second-class citizens, of which molestation is an acceptable behaviour for privileged bad boys.

Let me share an idea on this President's 2016 election. I believe the American people wanted governmental change to modernize, be robust, to improve and be more humanistic in its approach. The only way a voter could influence a significant shift was to create a chaotic state. The President elect was the chaos required to stimulate the belief in a free democratic nation where each vote matters.

The above positions force me to assess my understanding and review it with you. I believe these events provide a bigger picture of how **motivation** has driven the Republican Party. The **motivations** may be obvious and we instinctively know it, and maybe we shrug our shoulders and assume it is "just more of the same." My **goal** is to explain or open up ways for me, the guy in a kayak, to determine the **motivational** aspirations driving the selection of Kavanaugh, and the bad behaviour of a duly elected President.

I am not concerned about what side of the fence you sit on. Whichever position you take should make you reflect. Does it make you agree or disagree? Any extreme reaction provides an indicator of bias, belief, and **motivation**.

> *"Are the Republicans fascists?*
> *Are Democrats socialists?*
> *Our reaction provides a bias."*

The second example reflects on the decision to have Judge Brett Kavanaugh selected to the U.S. Supreme Court, and how it may impact my financial security.

I will interplay two items to present the story and make sense of the events. How does the selection of Judge Kavanaugh have an influence on my financial security? I am retired and my finances are tied to my savings and the resulting return on my investments. I do not have all the details or facts and will present a sketch in sound bites that reflect the environment. I use this story because my retirement is a significant aspect of my life, and I am making decisions based on the data I have.

My income covers my bills including chunky bills like replacing a roof or having a brief holiday. There are no disposable funds for global travel, or the other things I would love to do. I have to live within my means.

To sustain and possibly grow my funds I could:

- Get a job/contract
  - I would take contract work if I could do the job well.
- Start a business
- Write a book
- Manage my finances in a way that maximizes my return.

I was a partner in a small software company for three years. We developed product for two years and I hoped we could go to market early 2020. My gut said, not likely, as software actions tend to slip and slide. The term "soon" became oh so familiar. There was no revenue, only costs. As of April 3 2020, we failed and I closed down the business.

So now, I am writing a book. Will I have something useful to say? Time will answer that question.

Ultimately, managing my finances is the right answer for me. The **goal** becomes, "*To invest my savings in a way that protects me and grows, so I can live on a healthy income.*"

How do I figure out which business environments will prosper or struggle over the next 2-4 years? I will work with a professional financial advisor, and have him or her get answers.

What is the **motivation** driving me to make decisions of which my ethics may not agree?

I have to invest time to determine how the events in America may influence my funds. I will walk through the Kavanaugh hearings [34] and other current events, to provide my layman view. I will translate this into logic on how things might play out on where to invest or not invest.

Following is a summary to expose my **organizational** thinking and environment. I provide this overview here to set a scene. I provide the broader **organizational** piece for those who have limited interest in politics, or any idea of the Brett Kavanaugh hearing.

- My research of the U.S. history over the last 40 years, points out a notably long-term strategy by the Republican Party to "nickel and dime" Democrat failures and make them sound catastrophic.
- The Republican Party has groomed a number of people, one of which is a lawyer and judge to sit on the U.S. Supreme Court.
- The Republican Party groomed Kavanaugh.
- Kavanaugh is biased towards Republican Party views.
- He was the judge who stated the President could not be dragged through court, which made the President happy and his personal selection.
- The Republicans must get Kavanaugh on the Supreme Court in order to control the courts over the next 10 to 20 years.
- During the senate hearings, many of Kavanaugh's historic records were not provided for review.
- Three women came forward stating that Kavanaugh was not projecting himself honestly to the members of the senate hearing.
  - They made themselves known to the public and one provided public testimony.
  - Lying would be grounds for charges and possibly prison.

- An FBI investigation followed and a week later, Kavanaugh was voted to move forward.
- If there were no grounds to stop Kavanaugh's selection, when will Dr. Ford be charged?
- Does this selection of Kavanaugh mean she was lying?
- Will she be charged? I think not! Why? I believe she was telling the truth.
- The Republicans have successfully taken over the Supreme Court with a majority of judges propped up by Republican logic.
  - My question is how will they move business and social systems in the U.S.
  - The U.S. has a lying President who lacks comprehension of "the people."
- NAFTA[35] negotiation tactics utilized by this President were myopic and characterized by schoolyard bully behaviour.
- The global tariff wars have left countries forced to regroup, look for new markets and work to understand the confusion created by the U.S. President.
- China continues to take over the regions the USA backs away from, or shows limited interest.
  - China[36] is building the infrastructure to move resources and focus wealth. In return, they provide finances and education.
  - China is patient and will, as I see it, continue their expansion in an effort to become independent of the U.S. and European control throughout the world.

- In five to seven years, China could divert the currency of trade away from the U.S. dollar.
- Raw gold will provide a hedge against the shift in dollar value. Who is hoarding gold?
- Oil is still the commodity of wealth and a countries ability to support itself.
    - It is a resource used for building goods, moving goods, heating and a proliferation of other useful goods.
    - In 2019, oil was reduced in value because of over-supply and U.S. economic control.
- The U.S. dollar is used to control how oil is priced in 2020.
- The U.S. has turned myopic and self-centered. This may be justified.
    - Wiping out their own manufacturing base to drive pricing down stripped them of the ability to support themselves locally.
    - We want cheaper products and gaining efficiency will do this. At a high level, this creates a dependency across nations.
- Canada is a reflection of the USA. As a small country, we make great attempts at a moral high ground. However, this moralistic self-righteous view may cloud reality.
    - We do have an abundance of raw resources to be sold or refined into products.
- The self-image of Canadians is being stressed and the same narrow right-wing groups seen to be rising in the USA are duplicated in Canada.

- Point is, the world is big and Canada is small and moralistic.
- We get confused between moralistic beliefs at the costs of the majority.
  - It is not about stopping pipelines because of environmental issues.
  - It is about determining a path to better ways to heat, move products and protect the environment.
  - I believe pipelines are an effective method to move oil for the next twenty years.
- I have to gain expertise in the role of pipeline protestors.
  - How does money play into this affair? Who pays the protesters?
  - Who benefits if Canada constrains its shipping methods to supply oil globally? I would say, every other nation that produces oil or oil products.
  - If I believed for one minute the world would become moralistic over oil, I would have my head in the sand and missing the big picture.
  - We have the skills to find alternate energy sources and require a plan to migrate to the best energy options.
- A pandemic has flooded the world and closed down retail enterprises, as we know them.
- The lack of leadership by the U.S. government has created a confused state and a rapid decline in influential respect.
- The President is oblivious to the logic utilized to drive a nation.

- There is no **goal**, no plan, no vision, and zero **motivation** to manage the people.
  - This failure of defined purpose, as a federal government, may stimulate a rise in State leadership to discover better means.
- World governments have demonstrated an ability to utilize mass communication techniques, best known medical data, and to define and implement a plan to deal with Coronavirus. This is done with uncertainty of the effects of the Covid-19 virus.
- A vaccine to deal with Coronavirus is a common **goal** among nations of the world.

There you have it, a set of **organizational** items and a taste of the environment I present for my investment strategy.

I have lived with a cynical appreciation of large business, concentrated wealth, and governments. Today, I never thought I would be this concerned about my financial future. I need to get ahead of this or my nest egg may get crushed.

What would be the **motivation** driving the events in the U.S.?

- The President has been the smoke and mirrors guy, propped up on his own ego and taken to the cleaners by the back-room boys.
  - These back-room boys are men and women who collectively manage the Republican Party from within, or via their gifts of money.
  - They have set themselves up to ensure taxes on the rich are reduced, and public funding is slashed, because that is the "American way." It is up to each of us to make our way and prosper.

"What worth does a person need to join the back-room boys? Is worth monitory, moralistic or political?"

- More U.S. military spending to look tough against enemies who have already defeated them via economic basics.
  - All groups will build larger militaries to offset the U.S. military.
- Select white family dynasties of North America control money and power.
  - This is a myopic and biased view based of what I see.
  - Their **goal** is to ensure the collective team of the Republican Party are going to maintain and gain wealth, over the next 2 to 20 years.
  - Money means power and when Republicans control the court systems, they have a strong system to support their **goals**.
- Yes, they lost the primaries, but it doesn't matter.
  - They have control of the court system. Even if they lose the next election, their plan will continue.
  - The Republicans Party will return in the next election with another run at controlling government bodies.

Now back to my **motivation**.

- I am in fear of losing my retirement funds.
  - Am I going to have to work in MacDonald's in five years, in order to earn money to buy food? Yes, a bit dramatic but who knows.

- I need to readjust my investments to flow along with actions that fall out from the Supreme Court rulings.
  - U.S. medical plans will go away except for privately funded plans.
  - Military spending will rise in the U.S., Russia, and China.
  - The trade instability in Europe and U.S. will create insecurity on a global basis.

Is any of this true?

I am playing out a scenario that might help me grow my investments. Understanding the history, **organization** and plans, helps to clarify the fiscal environment. In most cases much of the data is available. **Motivation** to drive these speculations is screened or presented in ways the majority of people will gloss over.

The Republican Party leadership knows the real **motivation**. The President is not part of the leadership. He is the bad actor who runs the smoke and mirrors squad. His family and kids will come out wealthier, as they go along for the ride.

So where might I look to invest?

- U.S. Insurance companies that sell private medial plans.
- Pharmaceuticals
- Military contractors and Cyber power houses with huge mainframe technology to exponentially grow cyber spying and stealing of data and the protection of data.
- Privately funded hospitals in the U.S. as people will have to pay to use in larger numbers and tough governmental regulations will constrain any form of public health.

- The Democratic win in 2020 would open up more funding for public health.
- Food-supply lines and or food production as labour continues to move away from farming.
  - North and South America at a minimum.
  - U.S. wants to block immigration, which includes the low paid farm hands.
- U.S. water and water supply lines, as global warming ideology is by-passed by the U.S. government.
- Revamped retail logistics, as virus chaos is opening new lines of commerce.

I have the makings of an investment strategy. I will vette with financial people who speak their minds, study the world and the political shifts within our time. Inspiring information comes from smart money managers who know the game, and appreciate how world events rejig financial logic. Friends speak off the record. History will tell me if I am correct or close.

I have purchased shares in a company with advanced technologies to diagnose breast cancer. The company[37] holds patents and is in the FDA process to gain approval for public use by end of 2023. I have put my money into my accrued knowledge.

> *"My brain directs and my heart senses;*
> *I put my money where my knowledge is."*

I will need to verify my **motivational** and **organizational** skills to better adapt my plan.

Listed below are **motivational** items I have to research.

Personally
- Is my fear rational?

- Are there any real **motivational** differences between Republicans and Democrats?
  - Are they the same; adjusting to manage self-vested interests in wealth, or the concentration of wealth.
- Maybe my emotional reaction to Kavanaugh's appointment is just that, and life will move on.
- Is my bias about the U.S. President wrong, misdirected or right on?
- Do I want to be wealthy?
- Is money the thing that will make me a better person or a rich body?
- What data am I missing?

The Appointment of Judge Brett Kavanaugh and The Bigger Picture

- Has the Republican Party accepted the dogma of old southern rebels who have never recovered from losing the Civil War?
- Have they successfully created enough cuts by a million slices to get elected again?
  - This 40-year plan is brilliant in reality. Sick and cynical, but brilliant.
  - The patience needed is beyond the typical attention span; how do I prepare my kids, let alone their kids and myself?
- Are Republicans an example of the Roman Catholic Church?
  - They both accept that boys can be bad. I am astonished that I am able to create the comparison. Please understand I am processing what data I have absorbed and see played out publicly.

- The scenario affects and disgusts me.
- It is not the disgust that **motivates** me, but my attempt to understand the logic and how to invest to protect my family, friends, and community.
- Have women in the U.S. been slapped down enough yet?
  - What am I missing with this President as he belittles Dr. Ford? I would say the women cheering him on accept the rhetoric as a symbol of their support.
  - How will this influence business decisions? I would say sarcastically, investing in women's health in the U.S. is a no go.
  - Is this contrary or will the rich provide cash to care for women?
- Is the egregious behaviour of the few bad boys going to be used to attack all men?
  - The victim logic in reverse.
- The President is a simpleton and has no class let alone grace. At best, he is a lousy actor.
  - His ego is all that matters. Manage his ego and you manage him.
  - His inflated ego and interest in gaining wealth is his apparent **motivation**.
- Is the President of any use other than smoke and mirrors?
  - What value is he to the country?
  - Is this a model to emulate?
  - How does a twenty-year-old rationalize the behaviour of this President?

- If Kavanaugh's past bad behaviour, combined with his public defence, was not enough to get him side-lined, is it now open season on drinking beer and forgetting one's abuse of women?

I think about all of this.

I will read more from writers of right- and left-wing sources. It is a real effort to read extremes as they push away any semblance of common sense. The extremes of either side provide indicators of middle ground.

Summary

There you have it, a few pieces of potential logic that may expose **motivations** I have toiled to understand. I hope the speculation on **motivations** is clear as I drill through different topics; my monetary wealth tied to the selection of a U.S. Supreme Court judge; war and peace; religion and gender.

I believe I am open enough to constantly challenge my own beliefs and **motivations**. I want to understand how and why I react as I do.

I could see the **organization**, and the **goal**, but the **motivation** had to be determined. At times, my intuition is powerful and correct, and yet I have no idea how I know.

When the situation wasn't obvious to me I had to rely on my own radar. It might be as simple as, *'there is something good here'* or *'something is wrong here'* but I cannot define the specifics. It is a gut feeling.

"Discover your intuition.
Learn to trust your intuition."

CHAPTER EIGHT

The Tiny Picture

Detailed analysis of how I approach a new situation

Life is complex. I call my tiny picture, life.

My logic is functional; linked to nature and science, and relative in the bigger picture. There is the big picture of the universe and the extremely small world of molecular science. Humans fit along the spectrum, probably on the smaller side. "Tiny" is my reference to the size of me, among the whole.

Like you, I am unique and have managed to get to this point with no great fanfare. We have to define "great" and let the answer play out. Great is not God-like, nor the collection of huge wealth. Either of these items can be great. I am sure the wise among us understand their position. Great is what makes you great to yourself AND your community.

To narrow the scope, I will focus the analysis of the tiny picture on my history within the work world. Walking through stages of personal evolution, my focus is to find **GOM**, and provide examples of how I used **GOM** to help me in the world of new product introduction.

I recount this story to expose my evolutionary development and yet it could be the evolution of anyone. My story is small and humble.

On my journey, I discovered that I have to be my own first priority. It took years to discover this. All my education and upbringing has been around the support of others. To help others, to share, to be part of the team, to be part of the army or to be part of the management team. At the end of the day, if

I cannot take care of myself, how can I give valuable service to my community or any part of my world?

> *"You are your first priority, your ego is a piece to be managed."*

Self-awakening is powerful. It is not arrogant or egotistical, and yet it can be. This is about having faith in myself, my skills, and being able to contribute. As I matured, I began to define positions and paths that continued to test me and allowed me to learn. My struggle with humility and confidence caused many internal battles. Close mentors would correct me when my self-realization crossed into arrogance or inflated ego. The best mentors put me in my place with direct feedback. They played back what I sounded like and explained how they perceived my position. They did not beat around the bush.

As a natural introvert and a new manager, I worked hard to build confidence and gain strength in public conversation. I obtained training in public speaking and presentation techniques. The self-inflicted battles of introversions were being replaced with brief successes in open-forum talks. I grew to love public speaking. I have discovered that if I am **not** full of butterflies before a talk, something is wrong. Either I am not prepared or I need to get the talk rolling. The sense of success that followed public talks was exhilarating, almost addictive. Metamorphosis was both refreshing and foreign to me. I was learning to manage my ego, confidence, humility, and humour. I still have to work on these attributes, although I do better now than I did thirty years ago.

Today, I have opinions about many things. If unsure about a situation I have zero fear to admit I don't have an answer, yet. If **motivated**, I will do the research.

I understand getting absolute facts on global issues is beyond my scope. There are risks; I could be pulled into a myopic hole. Sometimes this is okay and results in learning. With other holes, I have to determine if I am down a rat hole and need to pull out.

The Internet is burgeoning with data and information. It is critical for a reader to have methods to approach the presentation and viability of the data. Methods are required to determine how data is made into information and then assess the value of the information. Gathering bias and the author's **motivation** is what I find challenging.

The published information has bias that had to be assessed. **GOM** helped by forcing me to ask questions and drill deeper into understanding the information and the author. I believe this tactic helped me assess the work critically.

Through my life, I have enjoyed meeting and talking to people. I can quickly assess where their head is at, and what direction I will take with the pending conversation. It typically comes down to me deciding on how deep I will go with the exchange. Mature people must be their own first priority, that way the dialogue can be one-word answers or simple questions; others may blossom into hours of good conversation.

"Mature" is a relative term to define the appropriate scale in all interactions. Maturity is completed visually and then verbally. You can gather details in parallel. The point is assessment skills mature as we grow into responsible adults.

The ability to read a person becomes intuitive and a bit of a game. Are your first impressions accurate? Accuracy of your assessment provides a measure of your skills to assess people and groups. I admit I love being wrong. Why? As a person owning cynical-based bias, I could over complicate reading an individual and create an on-guard flag, which stimulates further assessment. It is a pleasure when people's actions correct my cynicism.

"Maturity is relative to all interaction."

Be aware this can work both ways. I have incorrectly assessed people as good to go and watched as they corrected my assessment. Here, I discovered shallow people and they provide the greatest insights on how **not** to accomplish business or common **goals**. Shallow people take shortcuts, borrow other people's work, or make up plausible lies for their actions. I would have to find the point in which I would either build a relationship or manage the relationship.

It is in the art of understanding risk that people shine. Risk assessment is integral in all decisions.

I reflect on my early work as a production manager in an electronics factory. We used to implement little experiments on the night shifts when office and senior managers were absent. Sometimes we would cause an issue and discover we were in trouble. In one case, a senior manager brought us all together calling one person to the front of the room. He asked him to hold out his hand and slapped it. Then he laughed. He said, *"Sometimes it is good to ask permission, and other times it is good to just do. I prefer do."* Things did not go as we had planned but we tried. The manager said he preferred we keep trying. The message was apparent, constructive risk-taking was a desired attribute for young managers.

"Risk is a metric looking for a measure."

In business, there are defined rules or boundaries. The most sensitive come from financial rules and respect for people. All other rules are there to set boundaries and all boundaries could be explored. I define the work I did as a game with a brief set of rules and no limits. I needed good business mentors to ensure my exuberance did not exceed the capabilities or rational expectations of people who paid my salary.

My roles in engineering included the art of management on many projects. I focused on the future and present. Seldom was there an opportunity to work directly with customers, development teams, or field support operations within a large **organization**.

In the Maritimes, I was fortunate to have full scope of projects, which involved direct customer contact. I loved working with paying customers within an **organization** of 50,000 employees. Here, I was implementing new products for external customers. I knew I was in the right place at the right time.

I would say luck, combined with adventure and the ability to risk, joined the dots for my family and me. I had been warned that the smaller factories within Nortel would not likely survive and I had three to five years to do my best. The warning was accurate, and in the end I was responsible for consolidating operations and finding another job within Nortel.

We returned to Calgary where the Nortel business was moving into Wireless Telecommunications. Ultimately, I ended up managing the New Product Engineering team. I landed in this job through the deep need of the business to put "bodies" in roles; I was in way over my head.

I was fortunate to be part of the teams responsible for inventing or engineering new technologies. I was part of teams focused on the full life cycle of products. The span of which went from conception, focusing resources, development, and operations to delivery, customer interface, revenue and costs. Every team was made up of different members. I had to adapt and understand my position and responsibility.

I was working at least ten hours a day to earn an income. Fair exchange is the logic I use here to trade my time, expertise, and knowledge for a wage.

I was utilizing the "GO" piece of **GOM** logic and working on the third piece of the puzzle. It was in these teams where the bad actors exposed "**motivation**" to me. I could not figure out why bad actors would react as they did. It forced me to figure out what was happening. I was asking, *"Why did this happen?" "What **motives** did an actor have that were not apparent to me?"* I soon discovered the repeated pattern in the term **motivation**.

This is where assumptions can be misleading, and at times it led me in the wrong directions. Clarifying assumed thoughts was the way to get closer to the root of an actor's **motivation**. This applied to positive and negative. It was more meaningful with the negative, as it was contrary to my thinking and could add risk to the project. I had to be autocratic, but the gross majority of the time it was not by gaining compliance, but gaining agreement on ways to move forward.

"Leadership includes the act of following."

Was there a **motivation** I did not understand? Yes, many times. I could see that the term **motivation** was a broad topic and more mysterious to determine.

GOM was applied across broad aspects of my life, each time validating its quality. It never failed me so I could "bucketize" physical and mental attributes under the three headings. I needed to be close. Close was good enough.

I could work on teams and quickly assess the basics about that team. I was impressed at significant events that made a team larger than a functional group of people. Huge leaps came with recognition of a failure.

Teams I referred to as exceptional or dream team were often seen through the eyes of others who were learning to manage teams. The team leader would appear at my desk to define a spectacular event he or she had witnessed on a team they managed. These brief meetings typically put a smile on my face as I watched the eyes of a person who "got it." You can see in people's eyes when their confidence has reached a new better level.

When I entered a team meeting for the first time, I was running through the **GOM** process unaware of the players on the team. I had to be ready for people moving into new roles, and new members entering our teams.

I knew the **goal** at a high level; develop and deliver product **z** with a margin of **y.** Sub **goals** would be defined for members to lead their functional teams.

Organizational awareness would kick in, as it was more apparent and broader in scope. The obvious is obvious; it was integral to being **organized**. Our documented logic to introduce a new product was "common sense" employing rules for engagement.

The focus on time created the main metric to manage the team. This was a common theme for all who took part. Critical path[38][39] methods were applied to ensure a minimizing of overall timelines. In the world of electronics, there are unique names for this logic. The basics fall back to Civil Engineering, and how to order actions to find parallel activities and minimize schedules.

I worked through the following **organizational** issues as the team progressed.

- Was the **goal** crisp?
- Methodology for managing the project.
- Project scope and levels of complexity (technical and team sizing).
- Life cycle of the product.
- Project and product metrics.
- Capacity, capability, and control of processes.
- Estimation of and access to funding for expenses (labour, capital and material).
- Timelines to revenue ramp.
- Was this an above-board project or secret?
  - Levels of secrecy for the project and who can be privy to data.
- Was this product strategic?
  - Will it fill a gap held by a competitor verses being a mainline revenue generator?
- Was all information available or was deeper research needed to understand **organizational** roles.
  - Is data being held back?
  - Most members did not know how their work impacted bottom-line finances.
- Risk assessment in terms of technical, process, materials, financial, time-wise, human capability, and government regulations.
- **Organizational** structures of team members.
  - Functions and expertise levels.
  - Roles and responsibilities.
  - Team size relative to product complexity and timelines.

- Physical location of team members.
- Work environment – team members were responsible to their functional part of the company.
- Relationships between members and peer **organizations.**
- Escalation logic.
- Bonus structures for sub teams.
* Individual team members included gender, language, culture, belief system, education, experience, and their bosses.
* Who is in charge and who is really in charge?
* Seating position around the table for all people in the room.

One of my first items when teaching a new individual to manage projects was to respect their audience. Respect their time, and respect their role. I used to put my hand behind and above my head to act as radar, providing a fun way of saying, *"listen carefully and work to translate what you think you understand."* Yes, silly for sure, but people remembered my crazy hand gesture and in time, understand the importance of respect and listening.

Initially **motivation** would be taken at face value:

* To make money and profit.
* To successfully deliver product, satisfy business needs, and continued pay cheques.
* Each member is focused on the success of the team and the delivery of the product.

As the project progressed events dictated a deeper look into why a sub team was behaving in an odd way. I used my channels of people to provide insight: my bosses and their contacts including overall program owners, trusted peers, high-level contacts I knew, and their contacts. I also went one on one with individuals and/or their boss. I believe we might call some of them our spies and a normal tactic.

This information provided insight to be held in confidence between me, and the sub team.

Items I remember working through to find and understand a deeper **motivation**:

- Project delays were blamed on the wrong team, but driven by parallel management logic, to save their own bonuses.
- Holding a person accountable to costs that were part of their responsibility, but purchased under the verbal understanding that this investment was fully vetted.
  - Documented agreements were the one method that provided evidence to make large financial investments.
- Finding ways to direct blame at an operational part of the business.
  - Operations issues were easier to correct, at least from a customer facing perspective.
  - Having design errors could represent a broader and deeper failing.
  - This little nugget helped me understand basic logic to save face at a corporate level.
  - In reality, the operations teams were often the smoke and mirrors needed to buy time to correct deeper issues.

- Admitting design issues was the right tactic, but it had to be dealt with in a logical way that would save the customer from damage.
- Allowing a team member to take the brunt of a failure.
  - This created time to correct the root cause, which certain teams did not want to expose as their own capability gap.
- Incorrect assumptions by a member or team.
- Cultural differences not understood by peers or managers.
- At an individual level I had to understand why the behaviour of an individual was at odds with their peers or me. These items required one on one confidential talks and could result is discover of:
  - Illness of an individual or a close family member.
  - Financial concerns for an individual.
  - Religious beliefs.

Some events create wonderful learning experiences. I offer one story as it ties to culture.

An engineer working for my team was a project manager. Her heritage was Iranian and she spoke at least two languages with ease. Her ability to manage a project was excellent. She progressed to take on larger and more complex projects across teams that had various management levels integrated with the project.

A senior manager gave me a call asking me to remove her from the team. He was at a level higher than me and could dictate the action. He was also a peer I had worked with for many years. It was his contention that she was verbally abusive to team members during project reviews.

I asked this manager for time, and deeper details in terms of the issues and he offered to work with me to help correct the situation. I had no idea what was coming.

Over the next week he provided precise examples of what happened. I talked to other team members to gain their perspective, and listened in on project reviews to gather more insight.

What I saw was a sincere lady managing a project, but presenting her position or opinions in ways that offended team members.

I asked mentors whom I trusted for their advice. One did have an idea. He asked about her origin and where she obtained her engineering degree. She was from Iran and her degree was obtained in Iran. He suggested I research how Iranian women manage Iranian project teams. I followed this advice and began to see a pattern. Phrases she used to communicate opinions were direct and presented in a way that upset Canadian members. Not that Canadians are better, but certain phrases in English have alternate meanings for Canadians.

Our HR team approached the local university to determine if they had courses that might provide insight into Canadian culture. They did.

I called and explained what I was thinking to the manager who had asked for her removal. He agreed with my logic saying it made sense and gave me more time. He said he would be open to her approaching him for his perspective.

I arranged a one on one with the engineer to explain what I had gathered and understood. I told her about the courses at university that might provide better knowledge of our culture. She was upset.

We needed to make a plan because I wanted her to carry on with the project. Adjustments were necessary. I asked her to think about it and tell me the next day what might work for her or if I was making incorrect assumptions.

She went home and reviewed the situation with her husband, who was raised in Canada. She described what I presented, the phrases she used, and how the team was upset. Her husband told her I described her well as she had used similar phrases with him, and he would need to ask for clarification. He explained the phrases she used and how they might work in an Iranian environment, but the alternate meanings to Canadians would be offensive. She was shocked.

Next day in my office, we reviewed her thoughts and her husband's response. She agreed to take a course at the university and asked if I could arrange a private meeting with the manager who registered the complaint. At that talk she agreed to ask clarifying questions in future if the presentation data was not coming across correctly.

She had apologized to the team and explained what she was going to do, and asked them to request clarification of phrases that were unclear. This simple act would create a trigger for her to dig deeper to find her own understanding.

Two months later, the senior manager called to review. He was impressed with the performance of this lady and her approach to deal with the team.

"Cultures are beautifully different."

I would love to say I was a genius in solving this issue, but that is not the case. It was a struggle to understand what could be going on. It might be a simple process for others, but I had to get multiple inputs from observers to understand the **motivations** affecting the performance of this lady. I was happy with the results for this manager and the project. I remember thinking how amazing it was to witness this significant event.

GOM was working and I was applying it to situations to the point where intuition was leading me. The wiring in my brain was rearranging and I was maturing.

In complex meetings when my intuition provided a sense of something off-kilter, I would rhyme off the **GOM** logic. I discovered if data is unclear to me, there is a good chance the data would not be clear to others. The assumption that my boss knew more than me was an immature perspective. It opened me up to freely ask questions. My confidence was now tied to my intuition and a phrase passed to me by my mom. She would say, "It is great you have two ears to hear, now use your mouth to let us know what you think."

"You have two ears and a tongue...use them." [40]

Getting to **motivational** depths can be emotional and personal. It can expose hidden agendas, fear, pain, humour, trust, respect, and bias. The question "why" repeated a number of times is a tactical approach that helps drill deeper. When we cannot dig deeper, we have to go with the best decision we can make.

As we learn to manage the mass communication highway of cell phones and computers, we are inundated with data and various forms of feedback. The tools become addictive and should be managed in an environment in which we are learning. Boundaries have to be defined in order to grow an individual to the point they understand how the data influences them. Our education systems must advance to help expose bias in marketing and dogma, and provide a level of training that supplies young minds with better tools.

On a broader perspective we have to respect people and their time. We have to provide data that is valid and accurate, and provides enough information to expose bias and **motivations** not readily understood.

We are reasserting our **motivation** to better understand the world of psychology and mental health. A historical review of ancient societies exposes diverse beliefs and understanding of mental health. For the past 200 years, European settlers of North America have bottled up mental health topics. The physical world had jobs for us to do and this effort provides the means to be fed. Mental health topics have been left to private dealings within families.

It is with great hope that fear associated with mental health will subside and we will progress with abilities to discover another great adventure. I love the idea that we are integrated members of nature and I believe there is more to us than we comprehend.

"Time respects no individual.
Respect that."

> "There is a crack, a crack in everything
> That's how the light gets in."[41]
> —Leonard Cohen, Anthem

CHAPTER NINE

The Big Picture
My application of GOM

In the big picture I want to expose how I would apply **GOM** with a number of examples. I will start with topics close to myself as an individual, move onto recent historical events, and then tackle a piece of nature. Some are delicate topics, with dedicated members and I may poke at the armour. The poke is meant to be an outsider's view to challenge my own belief or understanding. I am not attempting to sell anyone on the topic, nor am I looking for agreement. I want to show you how I think through my understanding of life's events.

The examples will not be exhaustive presentations, but a listing of data I have gathered and used to make decisions or create opinions. It must include opinions, as that is what shapes the process and exposes bias.

At times, my opinions are incorrect and I adjust as they are corrected. This adjustment may force a recalibration of my position, decision, and/or action. I know this statement sounds too obvious, and the explanation may trivialize the whole process. To keep it simple, I am stating the obvious to be transparent.

I am limited in what materials I can obtain to validate facts and truths. I am not part of the details I want to validate, nor am I privy to intricate details that are used to create presented material. It is through this third-party view that I present my thinking.

The materials I have access to, anyone can access. Certain countries constrain access to information, which also creates a skeptical twinge about my own country. So be it, I gather what I can.

I do enjoy science and the study of great scientists who present ideas based on credible research.

There are self-help books, critical thinking methodologies, scientific approaches and forensic methods that provide solid research foundations. These tools tied to events provided nuggets of knowledge at stages of my life. A reread of material and/or alternative views opened new avenues.

Reading material must catch my interest or I will scan for relevant tidbits. Great indexes help focus attention on a relevant topic. Many books are scanned and parked for future consideration.

I have never been privy to intellectual think tanks, as I have never determined how to join. In reality I may not be at a level that would allow me to join. At Nortel, I was involved with the evolution of new Wireless products. A product roadmap is a deliverable. This was an honour and a privilege. The talent and passion in the room humbled me.

My mentors shaped my thinking and exposed weaknesses I had to evaluate. The weaknesses in my own logic are driven by lack of awareness, urgency, and my biased assessment of potential value.

Books, news media, opinion pieces, extreme views, biased reviews such as banking reports on investment ideas, friends, family and mentor input are the main sources I use to gather base data. If a topic is significant, then I dig deeper and read views as they become available. There are times I have reached out and talked to authors or people who present their position in public.

I love contrary opinion even when it sets me back. I will argue and debate with people I trust in order to flush out a good defence of my position, or determine if the new view is worthy of investigation. Mentors will push me at times and share knowledge they have gained. My trust in their data is in proportion to my trust in them. I will take on the contrary idea with new data and over time validate the work via alternate sources.

My quest at a superficial level has been to associate scientific knowledge to the ways we behave and think. A deeper, complex quest will help determine a link between science and faith. I do tire of the dogma of myopic groups that tend to be static and rigid in their actions.

Little has changed in the last 2000 years in terms of management of information and control of power and money. The digital era has created a disjoint on message distribution. On-line distribution is utilized to achieve the same basic **goals**. The ability of a person to manage the crowd has remained the same. Control the message and gather the flock in order to collect revenue or focus efforts. This cynical logic is not a revelation, but recognition that anyone can utilize the same tactics.

"Control the message to manage the belief."

I lived the evolution of the data-centric world. It started with a conversion of the analog phone system to digital switching. The data world grew with computer evolution, producing stronger processor power on a smaller scale. Internet, cell phone, and artificial intelligence have evolved as relevant tools.

Translation of available data into information and determining its value can be overwhelming. The complexity in terms of filtering or critical analysis has grown by exponential factors. Like children with a new toy, we have short attention spans and fear someone is stealing our baubles. It is the data flow and the material itself that we have to learn to manage.

The packaging of public media as fake news has created a manipulated disjoint in our time. It is a repeat of history, in a digital era.

A statement by the President of the United States to propagate chaos, amplifies the disjoint. Maybe this desperate man and his myopic party will revitalize voter interest. Or maybe the chaos will drive updates to the functional roles of government establishments and constitutional laws. My sense is we have to fail before something better is exposed. The pain is verbal at this time. Pain to the bone is needed to revive the appropriate counter force. We may be witnessing the fall of a once mighty nation as the pendulum swings to the chaotic side.

Let me move on to examples of how I accumulate data and package it to assess a situation, life, science, history and current events.

Employee Interviews

Hired as a manager at Northern Telecom (NT) in 1984, my career **goal** was to work for five years at this large company and learn how they accomplished business. My personal **goal** was then to set up and run my own business. My plans were benched and I stayed at Nortel for fourteen years, before I was walked out with so many others.

In a formal introduction to the business, new hires are gathered and indoctrinated over a period of weeks. At our initial meeting the individual leading the session asked each of us to define our education, history, spoken languages, and company role. I sat in awe as I discovered the majority were fluent in multiple languages. Being hired with people from other cultures is an eye-opening moment. This is when I realize growing up in Kirkland Lake with its diverse cultures is the way of the world.

In 1984, Nortel was expanding and required staff positions in production, engineering, support roles and management. People of all cultures and experiences were hired to create a multi-point view. Their intention to expand globally and have people live within other cultures was a key ingredient to understanding customers, on their home turf.

NT obtained the best candidate for a role and I do not believe I ever came under pressure to hire a specific person. Human Resource provided training to interview individuals. My experienced peers coached me on tactics for interview logic. We interviewed in teams. I worked with a team to hire my own boss.

I evolved to the point that I hired for heart over brain. Brain strengths could be assessed via resume, interviews, and reference checks. Heart strengths were defined in how and why they behaved as they did in their lives. This "heart" channel helped define the term **motivation** within the acronym **GOM**. The **motivation** for a person behaving in a certain way is not obvious and I love having an incorrect assumption corrected.

My interviewing skills evolved to a level where intuition was a dominating factor. After five years I had discovered a phenomenon I called the "10-second hire." If I was to predict with accuracy whether a person should be hired; or if I had to dig deeper to determine what set-off my negative senses; it would happen within ten seconds of the initial meeting as I looked a person in the eye. I managed this intuitive sense carefully to ensure I did not overrule the basics of a person's capabilities.

"Hire the heart. Teach the brain."

Goals:
- To hire the best available candidate for the position defined.
- To learn how to read people and understand their past and present behaviours.
- To train junior employees the art of interviewing and hiring.
- To build a team of peers who could critically assess individuals during one-hour interviews.

Organization:
- The job description and location hiring were available. I would be part of teams who were hiring across **organizations** and physical locations.
- Salary ranges were provided and based on role, educational requirements, and experience.
- I worked within the company position for salaries, bonus structures and benefits.
- Determine one's role within the interview process.
  - Was this a new grad recruitment event at a university or a public drop-in interview session?
- Was I a peer interviewer or the hiring manager with a set of interviews over weeks?
- The process for interviews over weeks was to select five to ten candidates from the resumes short-listed by Human Resources.
  - Arrange interviews and have the individual peer interviewed.
  - Complete interviews and meet as a team to assess our results and compare notes.

- Select the best candidate.
- Human Resources filtered resumes to ensure the basics were provided; education, skill sets, experience, and personal data as appropriate.
  - At times, I would be reading twenty to a hundred resumes. The ability to narrow them down was a learned skill.
  - Resumes with poor grammar, spelling errors, disjoints in time were purged or dropped to the bottom of the pile. I am confident this bias allowed for errors, of which I had to acknowledge.
- I looked for activities a person took part in, outside their work lives.
  - Volunteer work, sports, musical abilities, or whatever provided a tiny insight into the heart of the individual?
- Human Resources would arrange the interview schedules for all involved.
  - We typically interviewed in teams of two, minimum.
- Each interviewer had defined their set of questions that mattered to them relative to the position being filled.
  - Behavioural interviewing techniques were the trend. They provided structure and a way to obtain insight.
- As a corporation, we had no bias about genders, religions, cultures, or ethnicity.
  - I was privy to the understanding of cultures and religions and how different beliefs may create a path for the person to behave. Some people cannot work on Saturdays, some are team based, and others

are destiny based. This link to religion is delicate to deal with and important in any individual's profile.
- The exception that might bias a requirement is language. The person should be fluent in the language of the country where they are going to work.
- It was my priority when hiring that I meet the person at the entry to our facility.
  - That first meeting and my intuition would trigger the 10-second hire sense.
  - Body language played a big part of my perception. Eye contact, hand shake, physical appearance all ran through my vision or physical assessment.
  - I had to understand this bias to provide a proper interview process.
- The receptionist, security guards, or any person who might greet the individual are part of the interview team. This system included cleaning and kitchen staff, if available.
  - Interaction with other workers would help in terms of defining how they were treated, and could provide brief insight not obvious in an interview.
- The interview team consisted of:
  - Hiring manager.
  - Human Resource member.
  - Peers of the potential new hire.
  - Subordinates of the new hire, if the person was interviewed for a management role.
- One hour or half hour interview blocks were assigned to each team interviewer.

- The interviewee would have been informed that they would be meeting 2-5 people.
- We would gather upon completion to assess findings from each interview.
- We looked for common agreements and inconsistency.
  - A deviation would be a real issue that could be verified via Human Resources.
  - On the other hand, it could be an intuitive sense about something the person did or said.
  - The anomalies were intriguing. The oddities provided tangible queues to determine what was not sitting right with our intuition.
  - We could link comments across interviewers to provide a more refined assessment.
  - This did not preclude the individual but rather helped rank the interviewees.
- If there were multiple top candidates, the interview process would be repeated with different interviewers. This might include my boss or my boss's boss.
- In some cases, people were better fitted elsewhere, and would be interviewed by another team for different roles.
- I would then assess my inputs and select the best candidate.
  - They would all have initial hiring periods where they could quit or I could remove if the individual did not fit.

Motivation:
- At a personal level I wanted a person I could work with.
  - I discovered as I matured that hiring people smarter than me was good.
  - Early on, my lack of confidence and arrogance inflated my ego. This was modified with my own personal beliefs and company training.
- I wanted the best of the available candidates:
  - For my team's success.
  - For my success.
  - To cultivate future success.
  - For their success.
- Hiring for "heart" became the primary mantra. I could provide training for missing technical skill sets.
- 10-second hires were based on intuition and I had to learn to manage the bias.
  - Success rates improved with years of interviewing.
  - This skill was transferable to other aspects of my life.

Following are two stories exposing conscious decisions made and used to judge my success or learning during my hiring evolution. **First** is failure to hire the best candidate. **Second** is to define why additional skills on a resume are important.

Our business was rapidly expanding and we needed help. In my second year as a manager, I hired one individual to act in a technologist role. He was to trouble shoot and test electronic printed circuit boards. The "bone pile" of troubled printed circuit boards was large and growing. This waste had to be reduced.

The selection of available candidates was limited. We did go through the above process as it applied at that time. One of the Human Resource members was strong on a candidate. A peer manager and I were not impressed with his resume and even less impressed after the interviews. The HR person pushed hard for the individual and I agreed to try him out although my senses were tingling.

The person came on board and struggled with the work and his relations with his peers. I did multiple one-on-one reviews with him to determine what I could do to help. I utilized his peers to add more training. There were tangible metrics to define performance and we knew that with time, capable people could get the technical aspects. It was apparent that his electronic aptitude was low. However, the real issue was how he related to his peers. He created a negative environment for his direct peers and across the other two shifts. I was in trouble, as was this individual.

One-on-one reviews with him were not progressing. Any help I tried to provide was accepted verbally and ignored or rejected privately. He turned down training on interpersonal skills from our Human Resources team.

He was a silo unto himself.

I had to remove him. This was going to be a painful venture for me. I collected tangible evidence of the steps taken to help him. I was dumbfounded as to how I could have made such a mistake in my hiring.

I followed the proper protocol to remove him and then fired him. There were nights of no sleep, constantly struggling with his removal and my error.

My peer manager and I reviewed how we got here. We had both been on the same page and had doubts about hiring this person. We then approached the Human Resource person. She told us the individual was a next-door neighbour and his dad was an executive at another company. The dad was eager to find work for his son. Our Human Resources person believed the candidate was acceptable and we brought him in. She discovered in parallel that there were issues with interpersonal skills as she attempted to get to know him as a neighbour.

The three of us realized that we were in a desperate situation and that we needed help. This self-inflicted pressure allowed us to step outside our own logic in the hiring of the best person. As bad as this situation was for the individual, it was a learning moment in the art of hiring and interviewing for me. It was my mistake and two of us paid the price.

It was a simple point to correct and we agreed that it was better to struggle with tangible issues than to hire in haste.

In reviewing resumes of summer students to work with a group of project managers, I found an individual with definite promise. Students hired would be focused on documenting minutes, managing time lines, and updating metrics.

The individual that caught my eye was in the science program at the local university.

Her resume showed that she was a varsity volleyball player and a concert violinist with the local city philharmonic orchestra. I had to meet this person.

I brought her in for an interview and would have hired her on the spot. Everything was positive. I was impressed with this individual and her ability to juggle sports, music and academics. The interviews went well, but I lost the competition to hire her. She had numerous offers from other companies, and from other groups within our building.

In my assessment, this was the first time where I noted the additional skills section and the contrast of my personal beliefs. How could a person be good at all of these things? There are people who have talents and mentors that build better people. Was she lucky? I would say that luck comes easier to those who try harder, work harder, and learn harder. They correct their mistakes and move on. This young lady had **goals** and was **organized** to accomplish her **goals**. Her interpersonal skills made her a model candidate with heart.

> *"Luck comes easier to those who try harder, work harder, learn harder, correct their mistakes and move on."*

Roman Catholic Church and Bad Boy Priests

Moving up a level I want to provide a view of a recent event. The topic is tied to the Roman Catholic Church and Pope Francis's published paper on the bad behaviour of priests in Pennsylvania, USA.

A grand jury [42] report provides "credible allegations against over 300 Catholic predator priests." [43] The hierarchy of church leaders covered up the abuse. A thousand children were victims and there are probably more. The grand jury report can be obtained on line.

In response, Pope Francis filed a letter to the public to address this finding. Below is the beginning of the pontiff's letter [44]. The full text is available on line.

Letter of His Holiness Pope Francis

To the People of God

"If one member suffers, all suffer together with it" (1 Corinthians 12:26). These words of Saint Paul forcefully echo in my heart as I acknowledge once more the suffering endured by many minors due to sexual abuse; the abuse of power and the abuse of conscience perpetrated by a significant number of clerics and consecrated persons. These crimes inflict deep wounds of pain and powerlessness primarily among the victims, but also in their family members and in the larger community of believers and nonbelievers alike" [44].

"Am I my brother's keeper?" [45]

(Genesis 4:9)

This scripture provides a quote back to the Pope's letter. It is a question, which he and his **organization** have failed to live up to.

My intent here is to provide a recent event along with my interpretation and opinions. I want to expose my thinking. I will be watching to assess credibility of both the Pope and the Catholic Church.

Goals:

- To understand how the priests were able to get away with "bad" behaviour for so long.
  - To make sense of this bad behaviour.

- If this represented the finding of one state, what are the implications for the United States and Canada?
- To assess the Pope and Roman Catholic Church behaviour after this admission.
- To compare parallel events in our time and our history.
- To create my own opinion of how this issue could be corrected.
- To provide self-reflection of my own beliefs.

Organization:
- The Roman Catholic Church is a global **organization**. Its history, purpose for being, financial make up, power, and beliefs can all be researched.
- As a kid, I had friends who were Roman Catholic and through their eyes I gained a tiny insight into the Catholic Church.
- I had little first-hand experience working with the Catholic Church in any community. As a teenager, I sold pop and chips at bingo games in the basement of a French Catholic Church.
- I exercise cynicism with churches of all religions. I am especially cynical of groups who collect and call themselves a religion in order to gain tax incentives.
- I see the good in gathering as a community with common beliefs. I also see the bad in how members can be managed into mental and financial submission.
- I see the ways in which old documents are translated. Translations can be wrong or misunderstood. We cannot understand the author's purpose and **motivations** at the time of writing.
- I wonder what data has been left out of published Bibles.

- In the case of the Catholic Church, it is a male dominated hierarchy.
  - A pyramid scheme is a parallel example.
  - Women are allowed to follow and be members at fixed positions but never to rise in the ranks or be a Pope.
- Huge wealth has been collected and idols have been built to carry on a propagation of the identity of the church.
- I see "in the camp" and "not in the camp" bigotry.
  - History shows this to be a powerful tool used to gather flocks and revenue. *"Either you are with us or you are not."* If not, you could be an outcast, stoned, or burned at the stake.
- Raised in the United Church I could see it followed similar logic with variants in the acting model.
- I was perplexed by the lack of linkage between religion and science.
  - Are they different or are they one in the same?
  - Are written Bibles documented stories of the time? Are they witnesses to events that surmount our current understanding or were they tales written to create a mystic power?
- I see parallels with all church group logic, fixed beliefs, fear, and lack of scientific assessment to support their being.
  - They collect souls to raise revenue.
- The best examples of the worst positions are television evangelists who gain independent wealth because they dramatize and communicate a message.

- TV Evangelists have taken the church to the audience and gained independent wealth.
  - Two examples include Kenneth Copeland and Pat Robertson who have estimated net-worth of $300MUS[46] and $100MUS[47] respectively.
  - The hypocrisy is disgusting.
- Mother Theresa, Mahatma Gandhi, Dalai Lama are examples of great evangelists.
- Wars have been fought between religions.
- Religion was used to "purify" a dogmatic belief or myopic interpretation of historic writings.
- I believe that denying a priest the right to marry is wrong for a number of reasons.
  - How can they promote marriage and the propagation of children without knowing firsthand what this entailed?
  - Priests are men and men have needs.
- I thought about these things, as I became familiar with the operation of Catholic beliefs and history.
- Growing up I had zero suspicion that there could be bad actors associated with the church.
- It took me years to understand the church business model and "reason to be."
  - I understood their basics in terms of **GOM** but struggled with the **motivational** parts, as more wrong doings were exposed. This exposure coupled with their historic power created a suspicion that they had deeper issues.

- The Pope's written public letter exposed once and for all that the Church knew about the abuse of children for a long time.
  - How long they were aware, is known to the senior managers within its ranks.
  - They have systemically covered their tracks.
- The letter is released during the reign of a U.S. President who lies and captures global attention as a showman talking head.
  - Timing for this event is perfect, as it will be overshadowed by the Presidents next display of egotistical self-importance.
  - Combined with the microscopic attention spans of the public, the admission will fade away.
- In my opinion, the selection criterion for priests has been wrong.
  - A demand for celibacy in any individual is contrary to mental wiring and built-in programming of humans.
  - They created a refuge for men who had aspirations that suited a life of celibacy.
  - The statistical percentage of men who sexually abuse children has to be higher in the priesthood, than any other parallel ministry profession.
- Many bad boy priests were pedophiles, not homosexuals.
  - The priests who abused children practiced pedophilia as a choice not circumstance.
- The Internet world can access the damning information instantly.

- The speed of transmission makes it difficult for a 1000-year-old business to adapt their message to new media tools.
- The letter presented by the Pope provided no plan for the future, with an admission and a petition for absolution.
  - This reminded me of the politicians who pray for the murder victims of mass shootings in the U.S. They deal with immediate expectations with zero hope or a plan of correcting the root cause.
- Historic Church teachings have been exposed, in terms of abuse of the innocent. This exposure opens up an entire set of suspicions for the church as a whole.
- The Church may modify their old boy club and provide priesthoods or a "Popedom" for women.
  - This idea has a one percent chance in a hundred years or until the Church experiences deep financial pain.
- I expect to see a revision of criteria to become a priest.
  - The requirement of celibacy has to be removed. This is doable in our lifetime.

Motivation:
- The fundamental **motivation** for what has transpired was and is, the revenue stream collected by paying customers.
- Why did the Pope wait until a public hearing shamed him into a public statement?
- Why has the church covered their tracks allowing the abuse for so long?

- Is the saving of face so powerful for such a huge **organization** steeped in its own history that they cannot repent and make improvements?
- Is it public humiliation? The flock might migrate to another church to support spiritually and financially?
- Could their message of transgression go viral and potentially drive the younger generations away?
- Are they short of priests to sell the message? The public exposure created an image that all priests had to be assessed or at least suspect in any parent's mind.
- What catastrophic event will shake the church to correct for their errors, learn from them, and improve future positions for priests and their customers/flock/parishioners?

I have opinions interwoven with a layman's knowledge of the Pope's statement and actions to protect the abusive priests. Top-level executives who manage the Roman Catholic Church know the answers and **motivations**. My position is defined by the data I have. I do not expect to know all the intimate details.

Church is one form of community. There is power in the connection of community and church. The church is a business that must be managed. The church modus operandi has been a historic model used to develop businesses. Like many businesses, churches have to fail before they can be revived.

My position is cynical to say the least. Yet, I have faith in something bigger.

I believe we (earth and the species of earth) are not here by random chance. I believe there is a tie between science and the biblical scriptures. What that tie is, will unfold over time.

I state this to ensure you understand that I am not an atheist or anti-faith believer.

The Honeybee and Their Hive

The last big picture example is the honeybee, and the hive. I view them as the first nonhuman epiphany that solidified my ability to apply **GOM** to anything. This decision required me to assess capabilities and pre-programming built into the beauty of nature.

I remember my awakening that all things can be rationalized to a point, using **GOM**. It was a revelation that forced me to see parallels to human relations and behaviours. There are things we simply do not know and may never understand.

I propose that the application of **GOM** to all things keeps your mind thinking and looking for ways to simplify the complex. To simplify does not mean to trivialize or belittle, but to understand how and why things work and behave. All of this helps me admire the beauty of nature with awe.

Goal:

- To create a shelter and home for a centralized community.
- To provide bees to pollinate plant life, and propagate food sources.
- To propagate their colony and adapt to their environment (winters, summers, fires).
- To collect food to feed their nation and raise young.
- To build and train their members to fulfill their missions.

Organization:

- Melittology or Apicology is the scientific study of honeybees and can be fully researched. I will present my layman's view as I saw it while working the concepts of **GOM**.
- See MAAREC, Mid-Atlantic Apiculture Research and Extension Consortium for a deeper understanding of the honeybee and its **organization**.
- The hive is built to support living inhabitants, breeding grounds, shelter, and food storage.
- Food is collected and stored.
- The biology of bees is defined with a queen, worker, and drones.
- Each bee type has specific functions and they are constructed in a way to optimize success of the whole.
- The queen has the ability to propagate life as she is protected and nourished.
- The colony has built-in biological resources that allow a worker bee to take over a queen role, if the queen is killed.
- The drone is there to fertilize the queen.
- Workers provide all physical needs for the hive: Food, hive structures, food storage and distribution, defence, raising the young, queen support, heating and cooling.
- Population sizes are controlled by adaption to their environment.
- A bee colony communicates among its members, which can grow to populations of 60,000.

- New queens are bred to split off and take a swarm of bees to a new hive in a new location when populations grow beyond a fixed level.
- They communicate food locations and future best home locations if a hive needs to split.

Motivation:

To answer the true **motivational** make up of a bee would assume I have supernatural insight. I will imply my thinking to define what **motivates** a honeybee to act as it does within its hive community.

- To survive and propagate the hives future.
- They are pre-programmed to serve a purpose of which includes the pollination of flowers to support an overall balance in nature.
    - This statement makes assumptions about the purpose of nature and how we as a whole operate within nature.
    - Each species has a different programming logic in order to accomplish its **goal** and purpose.
- Is there a deeper **motivation** at a bee level? I will wait on science to answer this question.

The honeybee and its hive were an amazing metaphor that helped me rationalize **GOM** terminology. Once I convinced myself of the power, I was positive I was onto something bigger than me.

Science is beginning to link our being to belief systems that come out of biblical teachings. We are not here by random chance.

This drives a whole new set of questions. It is my belief science will discover the evidence to support how and why we are here.

GOM allowed me to assess my work environment, world events and possible logic for what is beyond the world, as we know it. It has furnished me with a tactic to reflect on the obvious, and then to dig deeper into the unknown or less obvious. It has allowed me to dig deeper into the reasons why events happen and/or unfold as they do. It has helped me hone and trust my intuition.

GOM is open to correction. It fits into my world of cynical opinions and I hope it can provide a simple piece of logic as a tool for others.

GOM is my give back.

Poignant Point Five
"Free speech has a price."
—Brian Waldron

CHAPTER TEN
The Future Evolution of GOM
Wrapping it all up

I have kayaked my last time for summer and fall. The cottage is closed and the kayaks are stowed for winter. I look forward to the open water of spring to get back in my kayak.

As a spring and summer person, I see birth of new life and the full power of nature in these months. Fall and winter provide counter forces to life. Fall is a time of splendour with natural decay in nature. Winter completes the picture metaphorically to our cycle of life in the physical world.

A specific public event in the U.S. staged the potential tipping point for a great nation. It captured me in a way that forced me to figure out a plan for my financial security. The collision of that public event and my financial insecurity triggered a kayak ride to think it through.

As I rode the kayak, a deep-down intuition began to make sense, and my epiphany exploded with lateral thinking. I understand the need to feel nature, and be clear of the clutter in communicating overwhelming issues. At that moment, my mind was clear and my ideas, crisp.

I had a sense that I had something to say, and it had to be stated, for my ego, my beliefs, and my **motivation** to give back. The fear I had of writing has dissipated enough to allow me to articulate my thinking. Here I am on the final chapter and I feel great.

The metaphor of a physical kayak ride provided a theme to create this story. My out-bound venture provided uninterrupted time to reflect, and allowed my brain to realign my thoughts.

The little picture view collided with big picture events and a practical application of **GOM** came into focus.

I ask, why now? Was it age and legacy or timing? It simply feels right.

Looking back, I see I had a vision. I was **organized** with sets of details. Chapter one was written time and time again over fifteen years. An index was generated and ideas populated, but my **motivation** to complete was never at the right point. My kayak ride on that beautiful day stimulated a profound path and provided me with focus to write this story.

I have evolved over the writing of this story. I fought to remain simple and to the point. I endeavoured to ensure my bias was exposed. It was a difficult process to tame my opinion and comments in order to remain focused on my **goal**. I discovered that I could ramble on for paragraphs about certain events, which might represent a confused bias. Ultimately, this did not add value to my overall **goal**.

For me a wonderful editor appeared at precisely the right time. How does that happen? As my physical art of writing matured, chapters progressed. Not that I am arrogant about content, but the writing started to "flow." I found I could strip out jargon, wasted words, redundant data, and rambling down rat holes.

> *"I hope I have been 'to the point' in respect of your time."*

An acronym composed of three words **Goal Organization** and **Motivation** is the sound bite message of my argument. They are common words combined to form a memory jogger for myself, giving me a tool to assess any situation involving people and uncertainty. I love the logic of moving from complex to simple. I do wish I had understood this earlier in life. But then again, had I understood it earlier would I have written this story? Would I have failed enough to find a path that guided me?

Listed below is a summary of the nuggets of value I discovered and talked about through this story.

- **GOM = Goal Organization Motivation**. This acronym provided me with a simple tool to assess any situation.
  - **Motivation** is the hardest to uncover. It is neither public nor articulated in a way that creates a crisp understanding of why events transpire in certain ways. The question "why" asked repeatedly helps uncover hidden agendas.
- Getting close is good enough.
- Uncertainty with results assessed and opinions created is OK. Improvement comes with knowledge, wisdom, grace, age, patience, and respect of nature.
- Complexity for products can be defined in technical terms and design capabilities.
  - Complexity in managing teams of people can be defined mathematically with the equation of **C=2 to the power of n ($C=2^n$)**, where **C** = complexity and **n** = number of people involved.
- The symbolic representation of an operational amplifier provides a model to emulate the workings of an individual, team, or company. Feedback is utilized to adapt action and output.
- The mechanical structure of "teams" or communities is a natural process.

- Cooperation is a built-in survival technique programmed into our basic mental and physical make up.
- A simple measure of a group becoming a team is when the quiet or introverted people speak up in team meetings.
- Rebranding of old ideas with new verbiage creates a modernization of terms, with a potential to capture markets, products and group logic.
- The study of natural events and science disciplines can expose linkage between them. General Systems Theory [48] best describes this logic.
- Science is my foundation. As I understood the basics of science, management, and teams, competition and profit **motives** became more rudimentary.
- Humans have a brain that allows the free choice of a **goal**. Humans can change the **goal** and adapt accordingly. We are designed in a physical way to **organize** and construct a path to the **goal**.
- Men and women are equal in responsibility and different in biological roles and make up.
- Humans have variants of form, colour, experience, culture and mental makeup. Belief systems can be managed to a set of real parameters or fake assumptions.
- Chaos is good, as there is a natural, pre-programmed capability to create order.
- Contrary opinion is good.
- Quality is defined as a fair exchange. This concept can be applied to broader topics such as employment, bartering, or money systems.

- Errors and failures are relative. Failures are a means to accelerate learning.
- History repeats itself with different generations. This is nature's way of teaching the young.
- Humans are not a result of a random sequence of events. The quest to determine our origin is a great adventure that combines science and faith.
- We are on a continuum with the universe. We are one member of the infinitely large and infinitely small.

These nuggets, as I call them, are topics unto themselves. Deeper research and documented details allow us to gain knowledge and articulate stronger opinions.

The acts of successfully failing and learning have provided me the physical experience and wisdom to pause and write this story. I know I will continue reading and challenging my own beliefs and opinions. The issue comes down to available time, as that is the most precious commodity. There is a trade-off between the best value of your time and your actions.

Will I modify **GOM**?

Can I reduce it to two words? I could group **goal** under **organization**, but I believe this over-simplifies the current process. For now, my intuition says, **GOM** works.

Will I change a word? Possibly, if there is a more general word that better covers a broader set of sub categories.

For my work life and my current study of world events, **GOM** is close enough. It is especially helpful when the exchange of money comes into play. It is useful to study the behaviour of powerful people and the people you meet.

I can use **GOM** to assess everything from a rock to the universe. This is done with assumptions that allow me to make educated estimations for my opinions and decisions.

One extreme example is how to determine the **motivation** of a rock? I have to assume there is a pre-programmed logic that allows a rock to take its form and hold its form. It allows me to interpret by assumption that we simply do not have the depth of science to determine why a rock continues to be a rock. The assumption could be made that inanimate objects are not **motivated**. However, that would narrow the view and force me to define a boundary I don't want to make. I have decided it is appropriate to not place a boundary and wait for science to catch up.

My point is the rock has a purpose, and a **goal**. It is **organized** in a way to expose physical make up and properties. At a microscopic level, the atoms have a deterministic reason to create their presence in our physical world. Atoms may lack the horsepower to freely change form or **goal** and this may be one of the reasons that science continues to explore atomic make up. Once we reach a point we consider the smallest of possible particles, it is my sense that we will discover something deeper and/or smaller. The rock **motivation** is a brain teaser and it played out as an extreme example for me to assess **GOM**.

What is the evolution for **GOM**?

With all good learning there is the study of the past in order to predict the future. Is there a linear or non-linear link that allows us to draw an assumption about future events? In small bursts we can predict possible and probable outcomes. With science, we can manipulate higher probabilities for success.

Success is a relative term and has to be defined. Is a gun utilized to successfully kill animals for food? Is a gun utilized to successfully kill a person? Reframing the use of success, I can create a value system relative to our state of life. I will define success as a progressive state relative to the current and past positions. The term is relative to the observer and their perspective of what success means to them.

My point is that language is the mathematics of communications. The difference between mathematics and language is the agreed-to definitions for fixed references. A time interval of a second has a human defined duration. A millimeter has a predefined reference.

Language uses a dictionary as a reference and the dictionary can be expanded to redefine references. A mouse is a creature and a computer-pointing device. Through time, words and languages have defined items, stories, and history. Over the world's history, communities defined references for various terms. They also expanded the volume of words to describe new points of reference.

It is in the understanding of the true definition of language that bias is created, because we can never be in the same state as the authors. As an example, to understand the true meaning of a version of the Bible it would require all text be read with a dictionary that reflects each words meaning, at the time of writing.

Today, we capture language in text, audio files and video files. The collection of word-meanings is defined via dictionary, and in context, within video. Relative to a Bible created on parchment, a video may provide a more accurate reflection of the history at the time of capture. We may be able to distinguish the **goal** and **organization** but miss the **motivation** unless clearly articulated. The **motivation** would be biased by the author's view, and potential hidden agendas. The audience has to be prepared to understand that the presentation of any data can be reframed to appear rational.

The best example that comes to mind is the constant lying by the past President of the United States. This is the purest example of propaganda. Continue to repeat a lie and it becomes part of society's belief system.

I rely on **GOM** to assess credibility and determine **motivation** as I watch this President in action when he talks. I use **GOM** to determine who is really running the government and developing laws or programs to suit their **goals**. I constantly study the news channels, written works and worldwide political states in order to remain current. I do appreciate the fact that my study represents a small piece of the broader picture.

I have concluded that the past President is "a talking head" acting on behalf of a few men and women. They have been able to manage his ego to keep running cover for their actions. Their actions benefit the President so he is gung-ho to provide public talking points. He is the least credible President, when compared to the purpose of the U.S. constitution and the faith of the American people. He lacks the set of skills necessary to represent the people.

> *"The past President of the United States is nothing less than a digital version of historical tyrants."*

His "power skills" are built on a broken ego that utilizes the perception of money and fear as a ramrod. He is a digital version of historical tyrants.

The real question becomes, "how did he get elected"? I believe science can provide a piece of the answer. My assumption is that the American public voted him in and it was not a foreign conspiracy. People were bored with the "same old, same old" provided by the political arena of 2016. I believe we are wired in a way that understands at a deep level that chaos is a must. The resulting chaos will ultimately lead to a new and better order.

Intuitively people know there is something better, and/or the old logic needs to find a new and better meaning. Was the past President a better choice? Alternatively, was he a choice that will cause enough pain to force a shift with the future governing of the United States of America?

Bigotry towards women and non-Caucasians is on public display. Public lying and belittling of media creates confusion for all ages.

The President's public fear of immigrants has been used to create a mantra for a bigoted slice of his voting base. This model has been repeated historically and has failed. I would say the tipping point has been passed and it will take decades to rebuild. I cannot yet see how far the U.S. has to sink before the rebuilding starts.

I believe women will take their rightful position as equal players and easily reset a different framework for a more mature government. I believe this will happen slowly and methodically.

A balance of men and women with multitudes of different professions is the ultimate **goal** for current and future governments. Each individual will require the skills to manage people and public expectations. Professional employees can manage complex pieces of government. This complex material can include physical public entities, public communications, legal wording to craft laws, and a modernized constitution.

We have spent 100 plus years dividing science into sub topics. We are at a time when the science of the physical and the science of the mind must come together. There is work to do in many areas.

Mental health is receiving attention it rightfully deserves. Advances will happen within the world of physical medicine. To treat the individual, there are physical corrections that will help. To fully heal the individual, the whole of the person must be treated.

Here is a list of topics I will watch over the next ten years. I constantly use **GOM** to assess what I can and in turn, I develop plans and opinions.

- The control and management of data flow, with tools to validate information legitimacy and accuracy.
- How the Roman Catholic Church provides a credible correction for their abuse of children.
- The rethink and redefinition of governments to manage the populations.
    - The rebirth of the concept that governments serve the people and create boundaries to maintain an open and civil society.
- Native people emerge from the shackles of forced dependency, and rise to be the great people they always were.
- The evolution of cities to small towns. People will live and work in the "town" of their choice. The evolution of vertical cities.
- The next trend of artificial intelligence and its new applications.

- The medical and scientific breakthroughs with mental health.
  - The understanding of how mental capabilities may expose additional senses, beyond the traditional five basic human senses.
- The advancement of science to better explain global warming with the hope that the science is understood.
- The waste problem we created devastates our natural surroundings.
- Self-inflicted damage to our environment may cause nature to take a drastic step to correct. This could be catastrophic for life on earth.
- The stock market crashes, and the associated crash triggers.
- The next military actions or large-scale wars and their triggers.
  - How does history repeat?
- The realignment of men and women to fulfill their purpose in the world.
  - Respect for the differences and eliminate the bias of old beliefs.
- The rise of China.
- The economic entrapment of Africa, within their own borders.
  - Are they being lured into an addictive cycle driven by money?
- The discovery of how the earth was populated.
- To understand if we are alone in the universe.
  - I believe we are not alone.

- The scientific explanations of how an event can happen at the same time in different parts of the world, with no known connections.
- The scientific link between science and faith.
- To continue to explore our world, our being, our universe.

I remember a phrase that a minister offered to me. He said success is made of three attributes. I was impressed and I listened intently, because he had narrowed it down to three.

A successful person has three attributes:

- 60% attitude
- 30% luck
- 10% plan

I wrote it down and thought it through for years. As I advanced in the world of new product introduction, I began to see this little formula play out. The project managers and business managers would never admit to anything like this, but it was fun to watch and see how the simple logic played out.

Of course, I tied it to **GOM**. I loved the concept of luck. What is this luck? Luck is events that happen after a struggle to discover a solution, or a path forward. Out of nowhere, an event happens that stimulates a channel to follow, and you step forth. I saw luck come to those that worked hard, played hard, loved life. They were more positive, enjoyed people, had empathy, and joined dots freely. A new channel can be spontaneous or defined in an environment free of the clutter surrounding a problem.

Joining the dots freely is a trait I was raised with. At times my bruised ego constrained my desire to connect dots for others.

Instant gratification is addictive and an adventure of maturity to manage.

At work I was called naïve and that I "wore my heart on my sleeve." I discovered that **GOM** logic helped me mature. Mentors played roles that became apparent through retrospect. I have faith in me. I have faith in the majority. I have a belief that when you connect dots for others, dots connect for you. Payback is not always seen instantly. I believe payback will come or grow in different ways in the future. It is this expectation that stimulates my awe in the beauty of life.

Your quest, should you choose to accept one, is to play with **GOM**. I would like to know if **GOM** works for you. I would like to know where it fails. I want you to tell me how you assess **motivation**, as it certainly has forced me to rethink why events happen. It forces me to correct any incorrect assumptions.

Join dots freely and risk short-term pain. Patience will show a payback in ways that will place you in awe.

I will carry on my quest to better understand how I can contribute.

My kayak is parked for winter. I miss the waves, fresh air, and the peace and quiet.

*"Then as it was, then again it will be.
And though the course may change sometimes,
Rivers always reach the sea..."*[49]
—Led Zeppelin, Ten Years Gone

Acknowledgements

I have written this book to give back and to push me into the new world. I am not a CEO or movie star, nor have I climbed Mount Everest to sensationalize my by-line. This story is my act of falling, failing and getting back on my feet. I fought to find a tool to help me, help me. Is it myopic or meant to be? You be the judge.

Were there costs…what do you think? Nothing is free. Free speech comes at a cost.

To thank any one person or to offer thanks to one thousand would humble my attempt. Missing a single person would shame me, and my ethic.

Thank you to family close and far, you are my strength and heart of hearts. In my eyes you are the champions. This writing will never replace presence. Your patience and love throughout the years has helped to make this story a reality. You are the players who held me up as I wept, and kicked my butt when I flirted with arrogance. I play this story for my kids and hope in a small way it guides them. Love you.

Thank you to friends who have challenged me to keep moving forward. You trusted me with a life-long connection and that is a testament to your faith. I am in awe and I honour you.

I have been fortunate to have a family of mentors who saw something in me and played me forward. A brief moment, a forced minute, or extended hours found us in the conspiracy of life. I heard you and now I am doing something I never thought possible. To free the few mentors who cringe as I attempt to speak, I will speak out loud. To every one of you I say, thanks.

Molly Croxall CEO (Chief Editorial Officer) who worked to tame the beast. Without your wisdom and knowledge, this work would have remained a collection of ranting and unbound words. Thank you for your courage and encouragement.

Adahlia Neil, your graphic artwork is exceptional. You lifted the artistic level of this book to give it a proper and appealing result. Your excellent contribution is more than appreciated.

Brian Walsh is a comedian and writer, and a lifelong friend from Kirkland Lake, Ontario. I asked if he had a piece of humour or a brief story that I could use within the book, he crafted Poignant Point 1. All credit belongs to Brian Walsh.

Mark Kossek is a family member and stand-up comedian. I am grateful to Mark for Poignant Points 2 and 3.

Thank you to the Beta readers who provided their critique and opinions to correct my errors. I am honoured that 4 friends were willing to read this story and provide feedback. If only the story was an easy-to-read romance or a high intensity suspense novel. The readers challenged my bias.

It is intuitive for me to utilize the logic of a new product introduction process for anything new; like writing a book. It allows me to move from uncertainty to knowledge with tangible results in a systematic and scientific way.

This story is a poem of life in action. This is the sea I sailed. I hope your sea is filled with the story of life you tame.

GOM it. Sail it. Enjoy it.

Tall Mast

Hold of wealth, cover bound as knowledge,
cook, first mate and cabin hand manage.
Mates of ship are bound by decks,
calmed as one by crew annexed.

Tall mast sail parting fog in quest.
I stand up in crow's nest,
aware of past and danger aside,
not all are with us on this great ride.

The captain stirs to direct action…
"Navigator, craft our projection."
Dots of stars guide thru' tangled mess.
Off to place we do transgress.

Sailing oceans does open time to ponder
with wonder, if I am to know or go.
Forward ho! All hands on sail,
knowledge gained, we battle gale.

The story crashes into we,
fighting to get out of me.
As I toil meaning of our kind,
my thoughts and soul unwind.

My spirit bleeds word ignition
with intuition and recognition.
'tis awe, with bits and sums of pieces
captures us, a hero releases.

M.S. Molly did tame the beast, geodesy,
conspiring to untangle theodicy.
Classical sounds ebb and flow,
crafting sweet jazz voices sew.

Pain mends and builds nature's art,
motivation wins to share my heart.
Speaking freely, the price I bare,
a release I give, without fanfare.

—Brian R. Waldron

References

Introduction

1.) Mark Twain, The Adventures of Tom Sawyer, Publisher: Dover Publications; Revised ed. edition (Jan. 27 1998), Paperback, ISBN-10 : 0486400778, ISBN-13 : 978-0486400778.

2.) Samuel Beckett, Worstward Ho, Publisher : Grove Pr (May 1 1984), ISBN-10 : 039462064X, ISBN-13 : 978-0394620640.

3.) Source: LyricFind, Songwriters: Phil Johnstone / Robert A Plant, Ship of Fools lyrics © Sony/ATV Music Publishing LLC, BMG Rights Management, Website: www.robertplant.com Twitter: www.Twitter.com/RobertPlant Facebook: www.Facebook.com/RobertPlant Instagram: RobertPlantOfficial #RobertPlant #ShipofFools #Remastered #DiggingDeep

Chapter 1

1.) Stephen R. Covey, "The 7 Habits of Highly Effective People", (Publisher: Free Press, 1989, ISBN 0-7432-6951-9)

Chapter 2

2) Fall on Me, by Andrea Bocelli and Matteo Bocelli from the album Sì – Deluxe Edition. Released September 20 2018, 2018 Sugar S.r.l. except track #7, 2018 Reprise Records. Song 6.

3) Judge Brett M. Kavanaugh, Nominee to Serve as an Associate Justice on the Supreme Court of the United States Source and Details at https://www.judiciary.senate.gov/kavanaugh

Chapter 3

4) The Iron Ring, See https://www.ironring.ca/home-en/ Under the Web page "THE RITUAL OF THE CALLING OF AN ENGINEER". © Corporation of the Seven Wardens, All Rights Reserved 2020.

5) Fall on Me, by Andrea Bocelli and Matteo Bocelli from the album Sì – Deluxe Edition. Released September 20 2018, 2018 Sugar S.r.l. except track #7, 2018 Reprise Records. Song 6.

6) Judge Brett M. Kavanaugh, Nominee to Serve as an Associate Justice on the Supreme Court of the United States Source and Details at https://www.judiciary.senate.gov/kavanaugh

7) Video coverage can be found under the Hearing of the Committee on the Judiciary, "Nomination of the Honorable Brett M. Kavanaugh to be an Associate Justice of the Supreme Court of the United States (Day 5)", NOMINATION HEARING, Full Committee, Thursday, September 27, 2018, 10:00 AM, Dirksen Senate Office Building 226, PRESIDING: Chairman Grassley https://www.judiciary.senate.gov/meetings/nomination-of-the-honorable-brett-m-kavanaugh-to-be-an-associate-justice-of-the-

supreme-court-of-the-united-states-day-5

8) See Cannabis laws and regulations, under Government of Canada, https://www.canada.ca/en/health-canada/services/drugs-medication/cannabis/laws-regulations.html

9) See Parliament of Canada, House of Commons, House Government Bill, 42nd Parliament, 1st Session, December 3, 2015 – September 11, 2019, C-45, Short title: Cannabis Act https://www.parl.ca/LegisInfo/BillDetails.aspx?Language=E&billId=8886269

Chapter 4

10) Canada Awards for Business Excellence was created by the department of Industry, Trade and Commerce (now know as Industry Canada) in 1984. It is now known as Canadian Business Excellence Awards For Private Businesses https://canadianbusinessexcellenceaward.com/ ran by Excellence Canada. See the web site https://excellence.ca/canada-awards-for-excellence/

11) I. Iilyaa Nouvelle Prigogine, Winner of the Nobel Prize and Isabelle Stengers, Order Out of Chaos: Man's New Dialogue with Nature, Paperback – April 1 1984.

12) Ludwig von Bertalanffy, General System Theory: Foundations, Development, Applications, 1968, New York: George Braziller, revised edition 1976: ISBN 0-8076-0453-4

13) Anatol Rapoport, General System Theory. Essential Concepts and Applications, 1986, Abacus, Tunbridge Wells.

14) Anatol Rapoport, General System Theory. Essential Concepts and Applications, 1986, Abacus, Tunbridge Wells, Chapter 5, Goal-Directedness.

15) Anatol Rapoport, General System Theory. Essential Concepts and Applications, 1986, Abacus, Tunbridge Wells, Chapter 4, Organization.

16) Anatol Rapoport, General System Theory. Essential Concepts and Applications, 1986, Abacus, Tunbridge Wells. Chapter 3, Recognition and Preservation of Identity.

17) Stephen R. Covey, "The 7 Habits of Highly Effective People", (Publisher: Free Press, 1989, ISBN 0-7432-6951-9)

18) The Iron Ring, See https://www.ironring.ca/home-en/ Under the Web page "THE RITUAL OF THE CALLING OF AN ENGINEER". © Corporation of the Seven Wardens, All Rights Reserved 2020.

19) Poignant Point One, Created by Brian Walsh 2021. Used with permission.

Chapter 5

20) Ilya Prigogine, Winner of the Nobel Prize and Isabelle Stengers, Order Out of Chaos: Man's New Dialogue with Nature, Flamingo. ISBN 0-00-654115-1. Paperback – April 1 1984.

21) Poignant Point Two, Created by Brian Waldron, Graphic Art rendered by Adahlia Neil
22) McLeod, S. A. (2019, May 28). Introduction to the normal distribution (bell curve). Simply psychology: https://www.simplypsychology.org/normal-distribution.html
23) Poignant Point Three, Created by Mark Kossek 2021. Used with permission.

Chapter 6

24) Anatol Rapoport, General System Theory. Essential Concepts and Applications, 1986, Abacus, Tunbridge Wells.
25) Ronald W. Clark, Einstein: The Life and Times, Avon Books, A division of The Hearst Corporation, Published by arrangement with World Publishing Company, ISBN:0-380-44123-3, First Avon Printing, December 1972.
26) Abramam Pais, 'Subtle is the Lord…', The Science and the Life of Albert Einstein, Oxford University Press, ISBN: 0-19-853907-X, 1982
27) Walter Isaacson, Einstein: His Life And Universe, Hardcover, April 10, 2007, Simon & Schuster, ISBN - 13:9780743264730
28) Dr. Michio Kaku, See his official web site at https://mkaku.org/ "theoretical physicist, bestselling author, acclaimed public speaker, renowned futurist, and popularizer of science." Per his web page, "About" as of February 6, 2021.
29) Dr. Michio Kaku, See his official web site at https://mkaku.org/ "As co-founder of String Field Theory, Dr. Kaku carries on Einstein's quest to unite the four fundamental forces of nature into a single grand unified theory of everything." Per his web page, "About" as of February 6, 2021.
30) Operational Amplifier education can be found on-line via "Electronics Tutorials" at https://www.electronics-tutorials.ws/. This site provides general insight and you can sign up for detailed data. Electronic Tutorials is a brand of Aspencore, Cambridge, MA, USA at https://aspencore.com/media/
31) Operational Amplifier used for reference to a learning symbol for humans. Graphic Art rendered by: Adahlia Neil
32) Bodanis, David (2009). E=mc2: A Biography of the World's Most Famous Equation (illustrated ed.). Bloomsbury Publishing. preface. ISBN 978-0-8027-1821-1.
33) Poignant Point Four, Created by Mark Kossek 2021. Used with permission.

Chapter 7

34) Judge Brett M. Kavanaugh, Nominee to Serve as an Associate Justice on the Supreme Court of the United States Source and Details at https://www.judiciary.senate.gov/kavanaugh

35) North American Free Trade Agreement (NAFTA) established a free-trade zone in North America between Canada, Mexico, and the United States. It was signed in 1992 and took effect on Jan. 1, 1994. Text can be found under the Official website of the Department of Homeland Security, U.S. Customs and Border Protection at https://www.cbp.gov/trade/nafta.

36) China has an infrastructure investment plan referred to as the Belt and Road Initiative. See Andrew Chatzky and James McBride, China's Massive Belt and Road Initiative, Council on Foreign Relations 100, Updated January 28, 2020, at https://www.cfr.org/backgrounder/chinas-massive-belt-and-road-initiative

37) The company is called Izotropic Corporation. Web site at https://izocorp.com/ I believe in their technology and the benefits it will provide to women. I started purchasing shares in March of 2020, as the pandemic crashed the markets. As of March 2021 I continue to expand my holdings. I do not act as a promotor of stocks of any kind. Any decision you make to buy stocks or any asset has to be done with proper due diligence. I provide this data as a reference for you to measure me with real data.

Chapter 8

38) A. T. Armstrong-Wright, Critical Path Method: Introduction and Practice, Longmans, Hardcover January 1, 1969 ISBN-10: 0582410401

39) R. Buckminster Fuller, Critical Path, February 1982, Publisher: St. Martin's Griffin, ISBN: 0312174918

40) A figure of speech taught to me by my mom. I apologize if it is offensive in any way.

41) Source: Musixmatch, Songwriter: Leonard Cohen, Anthem, from the album The Future, by Leonard Cohen, Released November 24,1992, Label Columbia.

Chapter 9

42) Pennsylvania Diocese Victims Report, Office of the Attorney General, Commonwealth of Pennsylvania, can be found at https://www.attorneygeneral.gov/report/.The Grand Jury Report can be found on this site for download and reading.

43) Report I of the 40th Statewide Investigating Grand Jury, Redacted by order of PA Supreme Court July 27, 2018, Pennsylvania Diocese Victims Report, Office of the Attorney General, Commonwealth of Pennsylvania, Introduction page 1

44) Read the pope's letter to the faithful on abuse in the Catholic Church, Article by Paul Schemm, August 20, 2018 at 7:31 am EDT, The Washington Post. Article can be found at: https://www.washingtonpost.com/news/acts-of-faith/wp/2018/08/20/read-the-popes-letter-to-the-faithful-on-abuse-in-catholic-church/

45) The Holy Bible King James Version, Genesis 4:9.
46) Net worth estimate of Kenneth Copeland as per Celebrity Net Worth as of November 06 2021. https://www.celebritynetworth.com/ https://www.celebritynetworth.com/dl/kenneth-copeland/
47) Net worth estimate of Pat Robertson as per Celebrity Net Worth as of November 06 2021. https://www.celebritynetworth.com/ https://www.celebritynetworth.com/dl/pat-robertson/

Chapter 10
48) Ludwig von Bertalanffy, General System Theory: Foundations, Development, Applications, 1968, New York: George Braziller, revised edition 1976: ISBN 0-8076-0453-4.
49) Source: LyricFind, Songwriters: Jimmy Page / Robert Plant, Ten Years Gone, lyrics © Warner Chappell Music, Inc. Artist: Led Zeppelin, Album: Physical Graffiti, 1975.

Back Matter
50) The Ritual of the Calling of an Engineer, Student Information Session, Camp One, Greater Toronto Area, Power Point Presentation dated January 25 2012. See The Obligation starting on page 21. Quote found within The Obligation by Rudyard Kipling. https://my.alumni.utoronto.ca/s/731/images/editor_documents/Engineering/iron_ring/student_information_session_powerpoint__jan_2-012.pdf?sessionid=a627c743-7b46-42d1-83ac-adcf523ea614&cc=1

The significance of the back cover photo

Every tree matters and the tall tree matters to me. It is twice the size of all surrounding trees, standing as a sentinel, keeping watch over travellers on the lake. A beacon of age, wisdom and strength, its height commands the robust forest that bows at its feet. The man-made sailboat destroyed on the beach, contrasts the secret of life. To view the approaching panorama from the kayak, ties me into the story. As an observer in awe of nature I see a set of metaphors linking this scene to GOM: One natural and one man-made. Everything has a meaning and as subtle as it is, this tree plays into this story.

Text References

Heinz R Pagels, The Cosmic Code, Quantum Physics as the Language of Nature, A Bantam Book, published by arrangement with Simon & Schuster 3rd printing May 1984, ISBN 0-553-24625-9.

Anatol Rapoport, General System Theory. Essential Concepts and Applications, 1986, Abacus, Tunbridge Wells.

Ludwig von Bertalanffy, General System Theory: Foundations, Development, Applications, 1968, New York: George Braziller, revised edition 1976: ISBN 0-8076-0453-4

Ilya Prigogine, Winner of the Nobel Prize and Isabelle Stengers, Order Out of Chaos: Man's New Dialogue with Nature, Flamingo. ISBN 0-00-654115-1. Paperback – April 1 1984.

Ronald W. Clark, Einstein: The Life and Times, Avon Books, A division of The Hearst Corporation, Published by arrangement with World Publishing Company, ISBN:0-380-44123-3, First Avon Printing, December 1972.

Abramam Pais, 'Subtle is the Lord...', The Science and the Life of Albert Einstein, Oxford University Press, ISBN: 0-19-853907-X, 1982

Walter Isaacson, Einstein: His Life And Universe, Hardcover, April 10, 2007, Simon & Schuster, ISBN - 13:9780743264730

Stephen W. Hawking, A Brief History of Time, From the Big bang to Black Holes, A Bantam Book, April 1988, ISBN 0-553-5340-X

John Briggs and F. David Peat, Turbulent Mirror, An Illustrated Guide to Chaos Theory and the Science of Wholeness, Harper & Row, Publishers, New York 1990 ISBN 0-06-016061-6

George Soros, The Alchemy of Finance, Reading the Mind of the Market, Published by Simon & Schuster Inc, 1988, ISBN: 0-671-63455-0

Charles Mackay, LL.D. Extraordinary Popular Delusions and the Madness of Crowds, Harmony Books / New York, 1980, ISBN 0-517-53919-5 pbk. Original work published in 1841.

Sun-tzu, The Art of War, New Translation by Ralph D Sawyer, Barnes & Noble Books, 1994 ISBN 1-56619-297-9 casebound.

Stephen R. Covey, "The 7 Habits of Highly Effective People", (Publisher: Free Press, 1989, ISBN 0-7432-6951-9)

About The Author

G**oal Organization Motivation** is my give back. It was created as a story for my kids as they moved into the world of work and new communities. It is a life of piecing together answers to create a simple model to assess any situation.

Photo by Lauren Waldron

I grew up and completed high school in Kirkland Lake, Ontario. Fishing and hiking were parts of my youth. I had a reputation for holding large house parties. Entry required a meeting with my mom, who never judged and used humour to disarm the age gap, a nugget of wisdom to teach the utility of humour.

Over 20 years, my parents and grandparents along with the KL community built my base ethic; care for others, hard work, curiosity and creativity. Science is a passion for me, as is, understanding how events anywhere might influence our life and finances.

I hold a Diploma in Civil Technology and Bachelor of Science in Electrical Engineering. Working in professional roles in management at Nortel is where **GOM** took shape. The art of introducing new products and managing people were keen interests. I considered myself fortunate to have worked and resided in Calgary, Alberta; Amherst, Nova Scotia, and Burlington, Ontario. With conviction I confess I found people across the nation to be "nuggets of gold".

I propose people are "perfect with flaws". Physically and mentally each person is part of a normal distribution. Perfect replaces the term normal where as flaws provide contrary balance. If the ego is in balance each person can discover who he or she is. There is need to manage the flaws. There is no need to be humble about you being you.

Mentors shaped me through my life and playing this forward is the wisdom of age. It is in reflection that we see how the many bits and pieces have influenced us. Grand failures create the quickest learning and when combined with the billion little things, add up to make a person larger than all the pieces.

I am blessed and privileged with two wonderful daughters. I work hard to tease my grandkids with my "perfection" mantra.

Meanwhile, I give you **GOM**!

"...Honour and Cold Iron" [50]
from Ritual of the Calling of an Engineer
by Rudyard Kipling

www.ingramcontent.com/pod-product-compliance
Lightning Source LLC
Chambersburg PA
CBHW032153160426
43197CB00008B/901